ADULT
COLORING BOOK
STRESS RELIEF DESIGNS

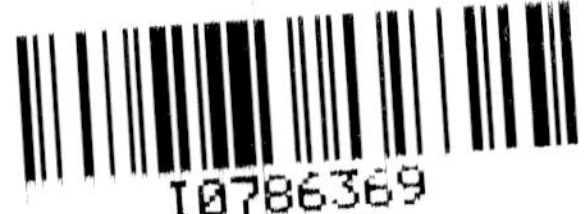

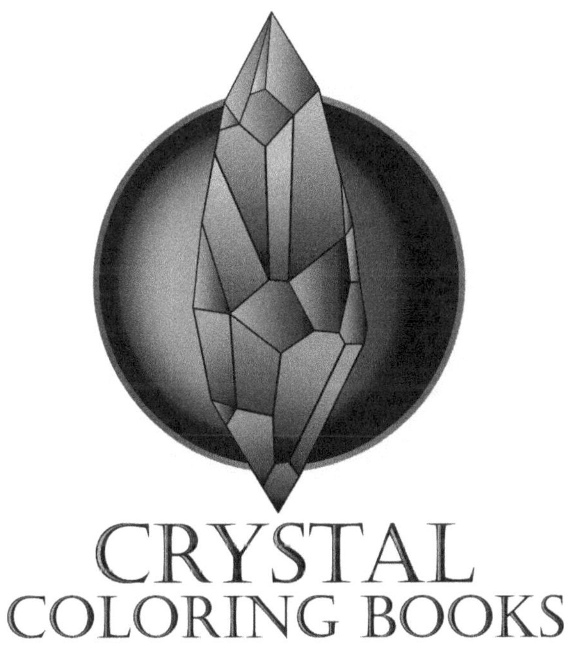

CRYSTAL
COLORING BOOKS

Copyright © 2017 Crystal Coloring Books

ISBN-13: 978-1721216093
ISBN-10: 172121609X

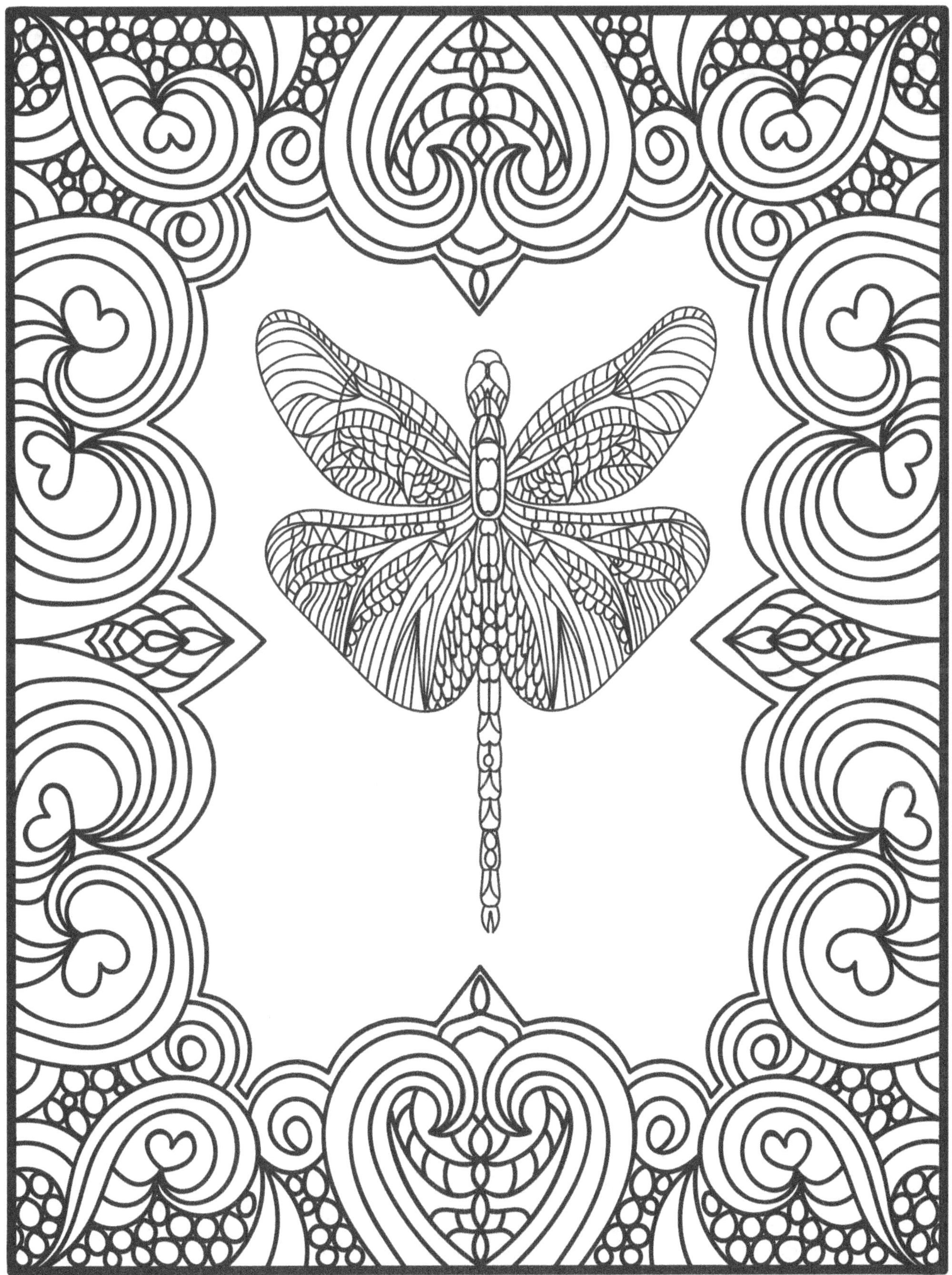

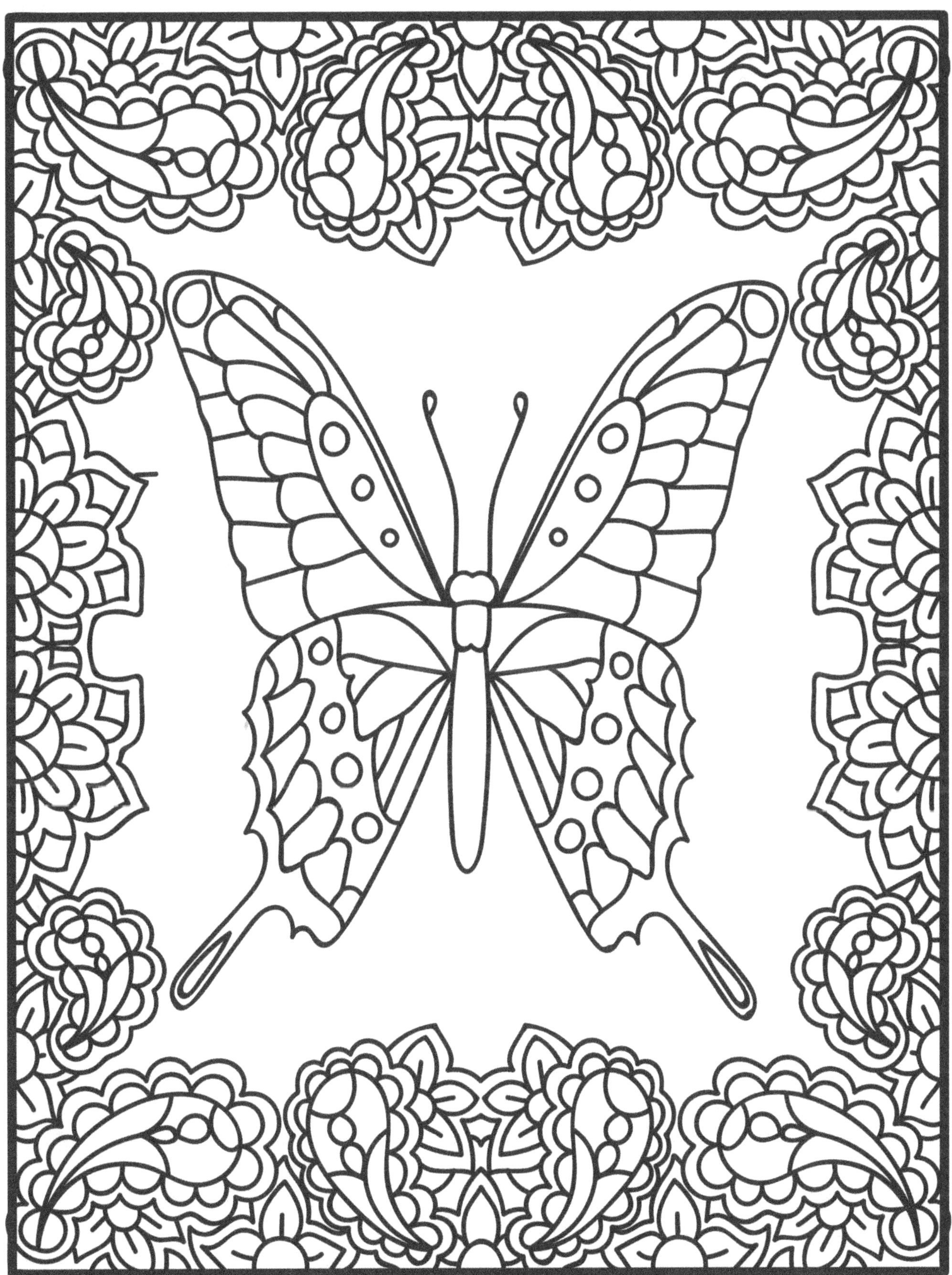

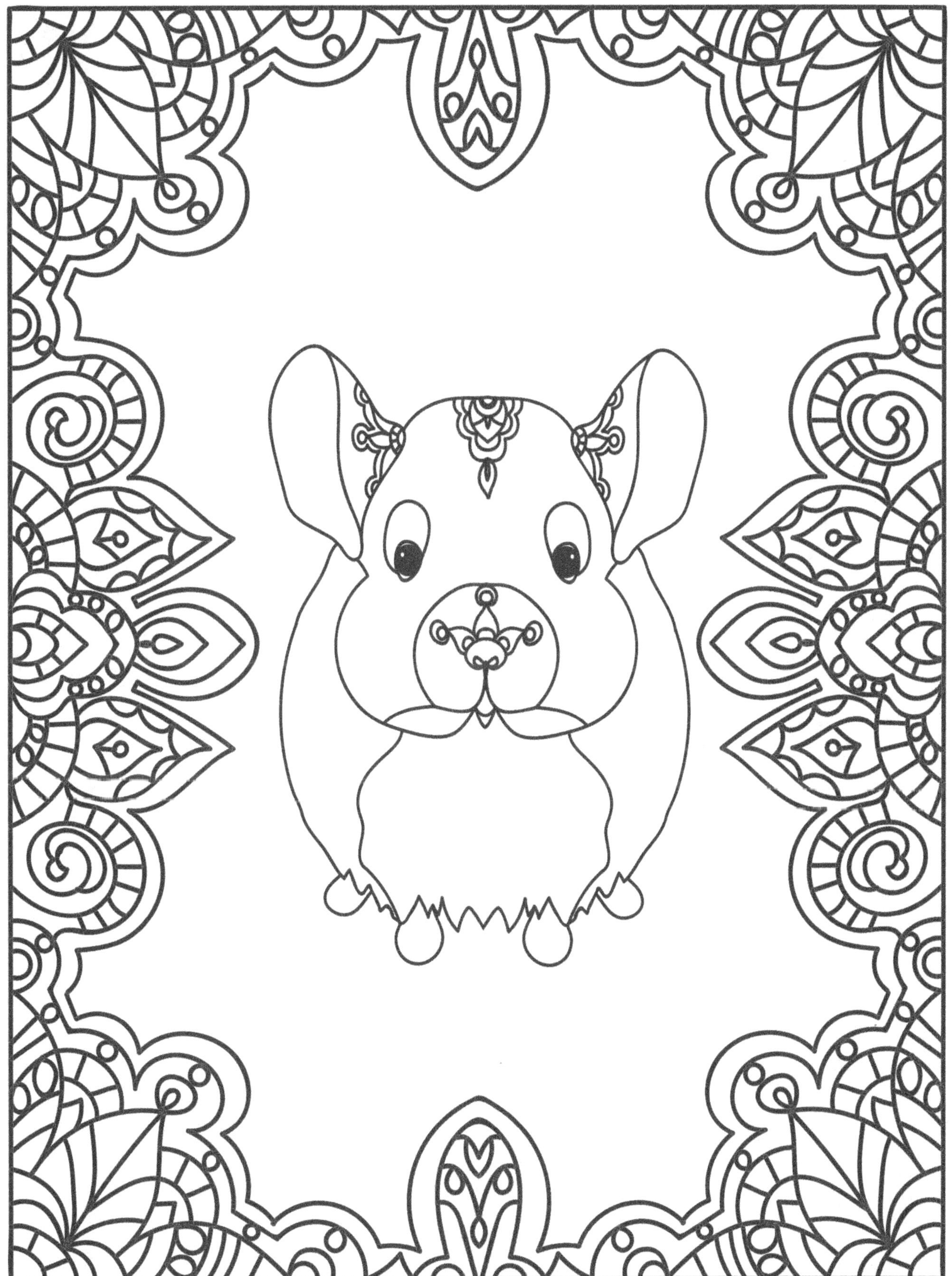

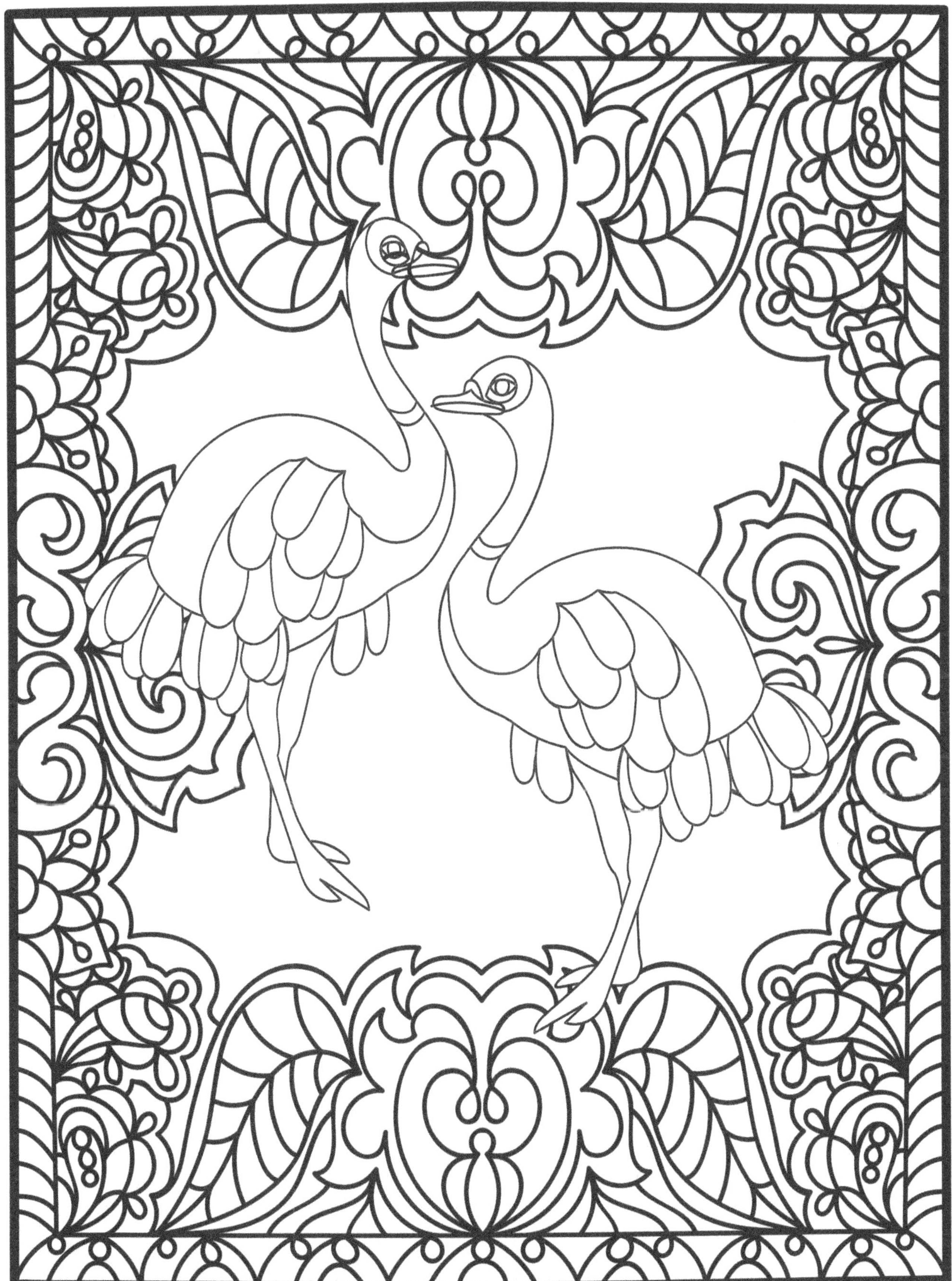

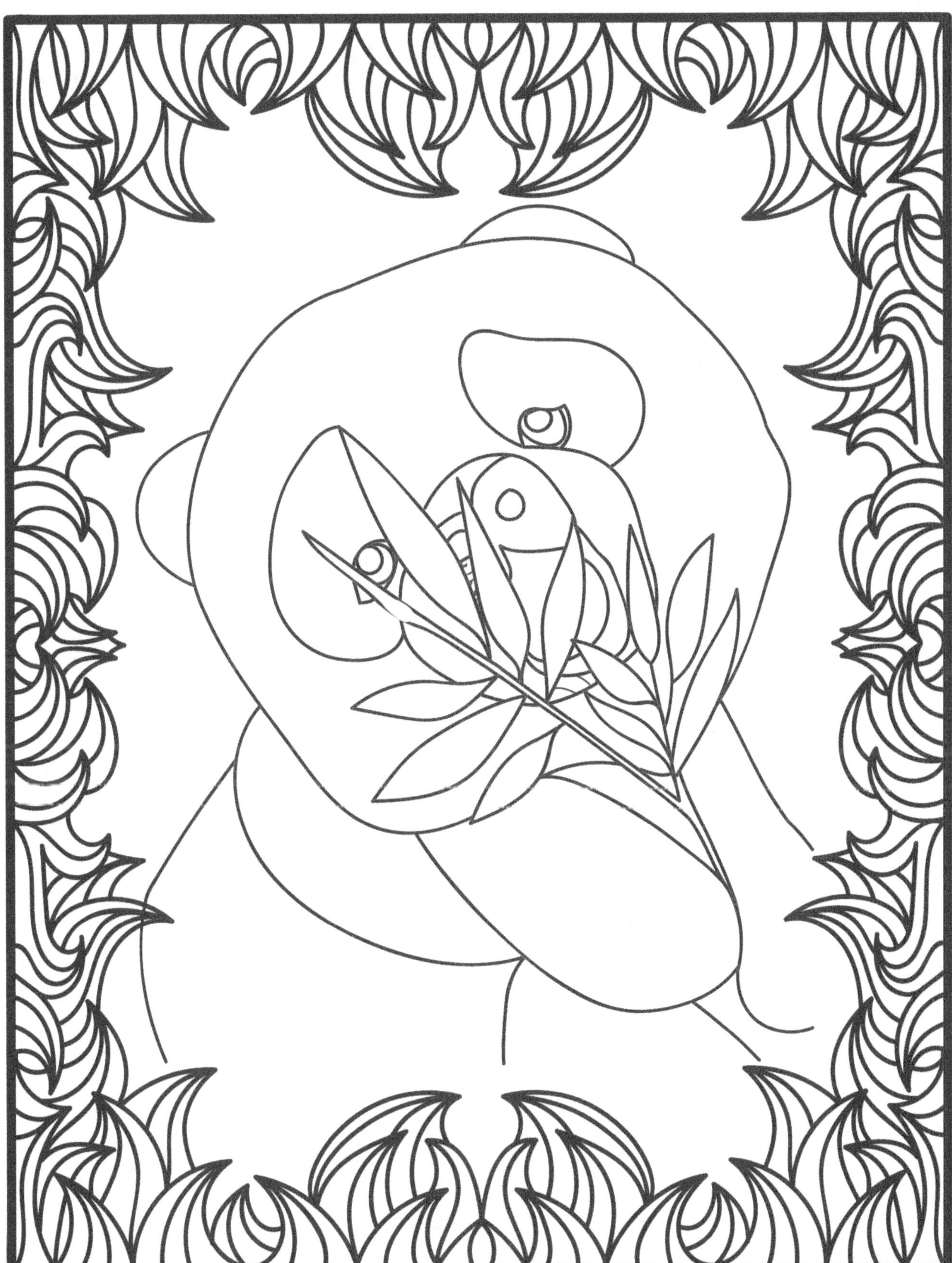

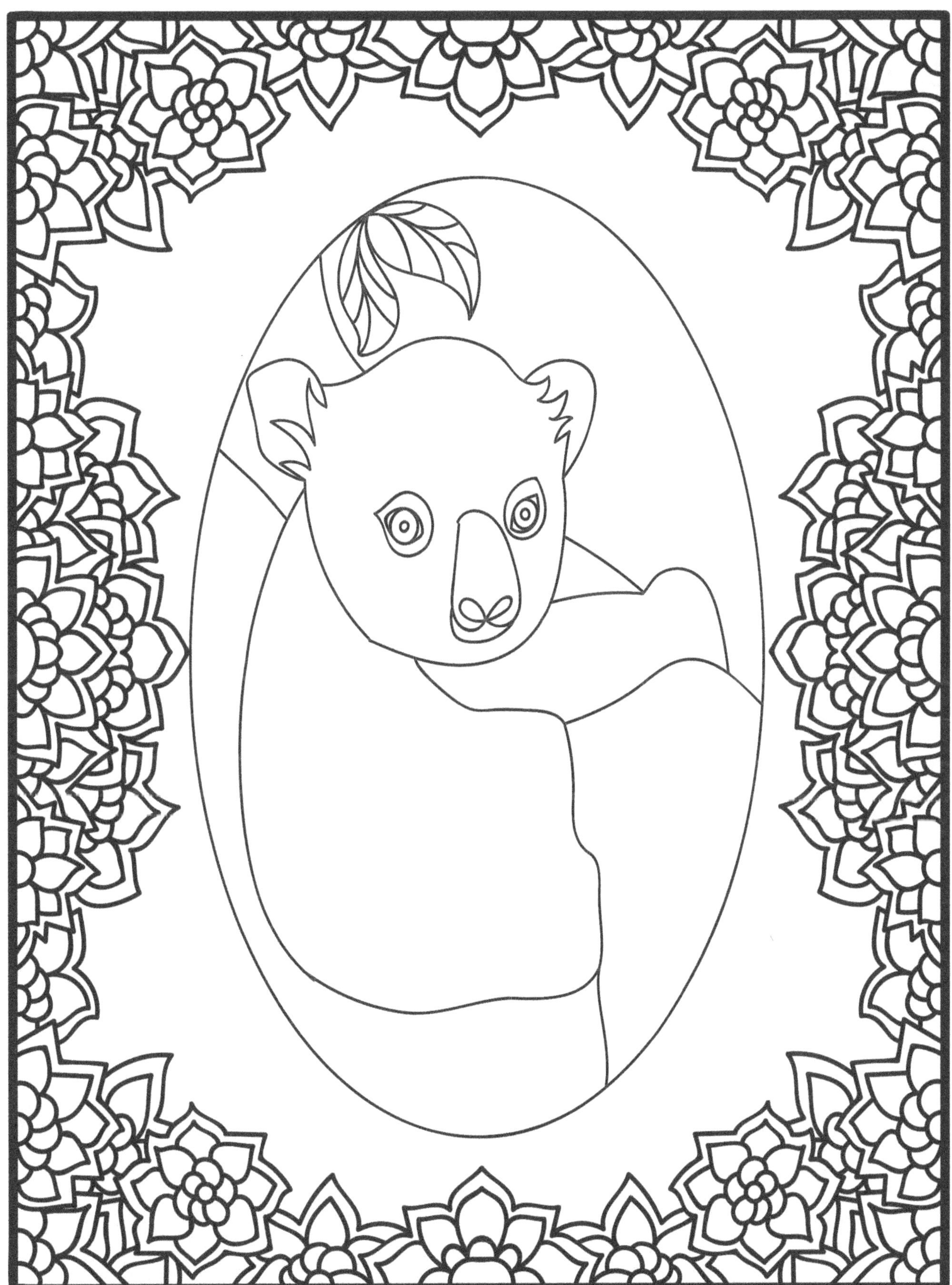

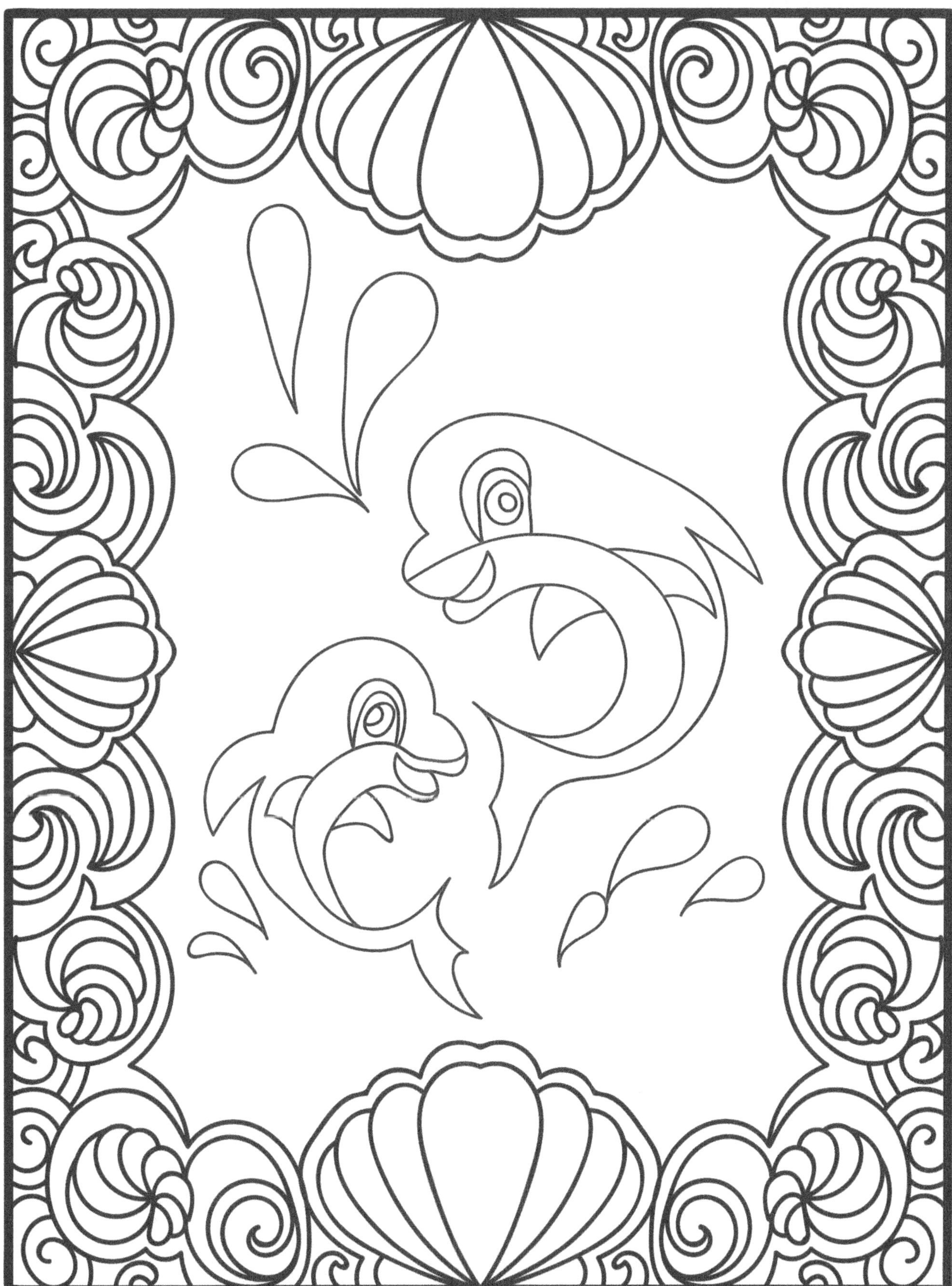

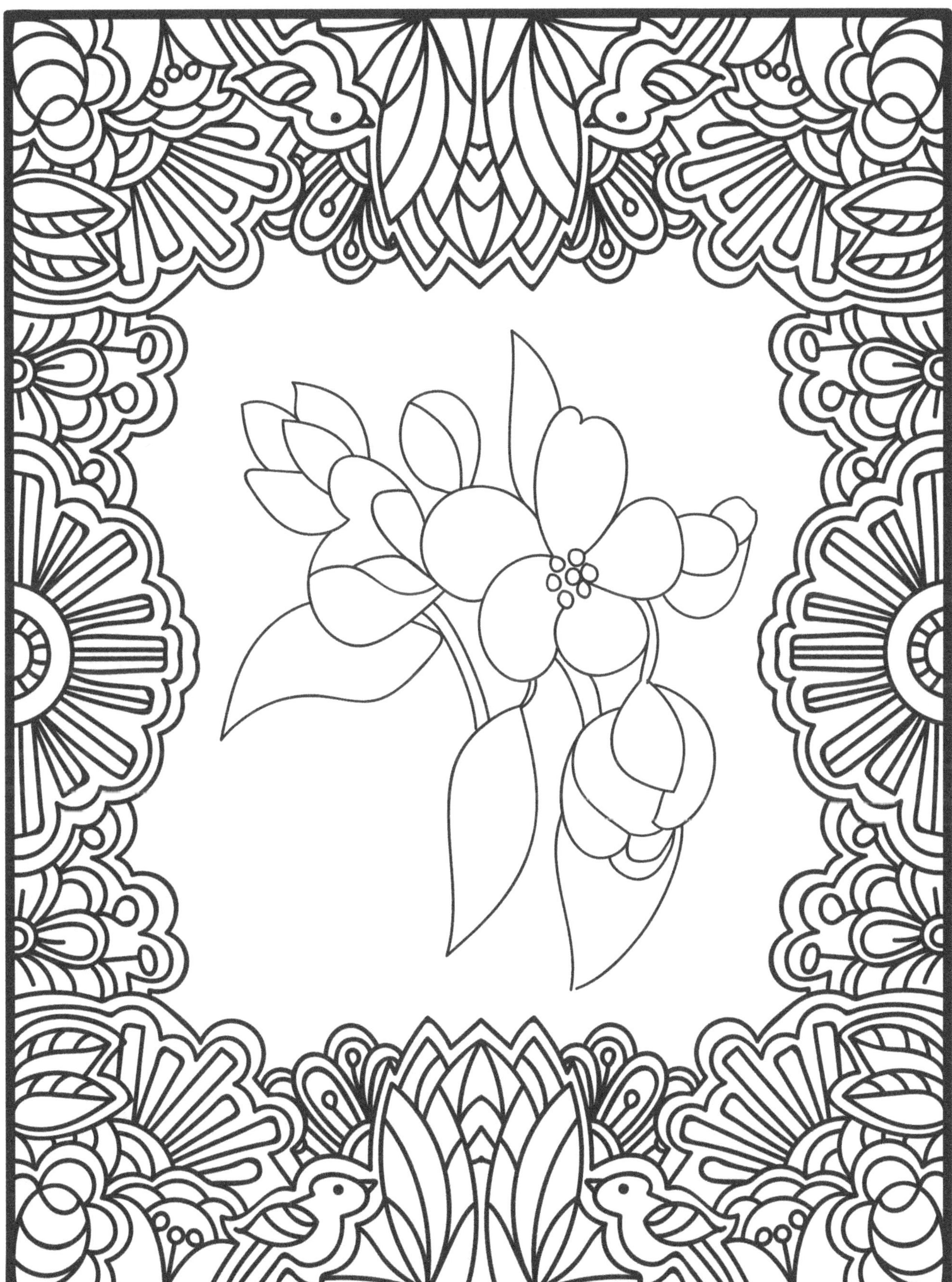

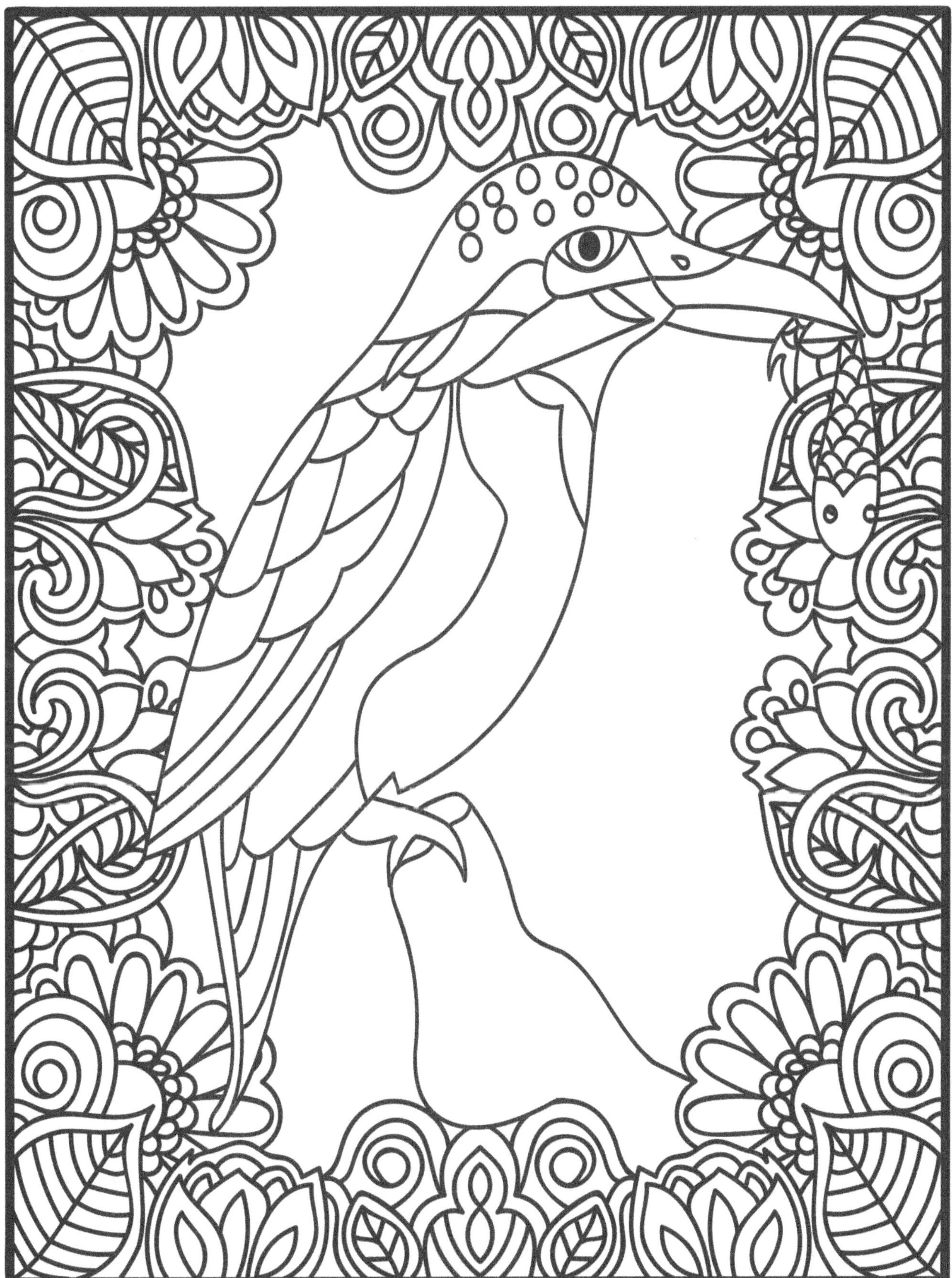

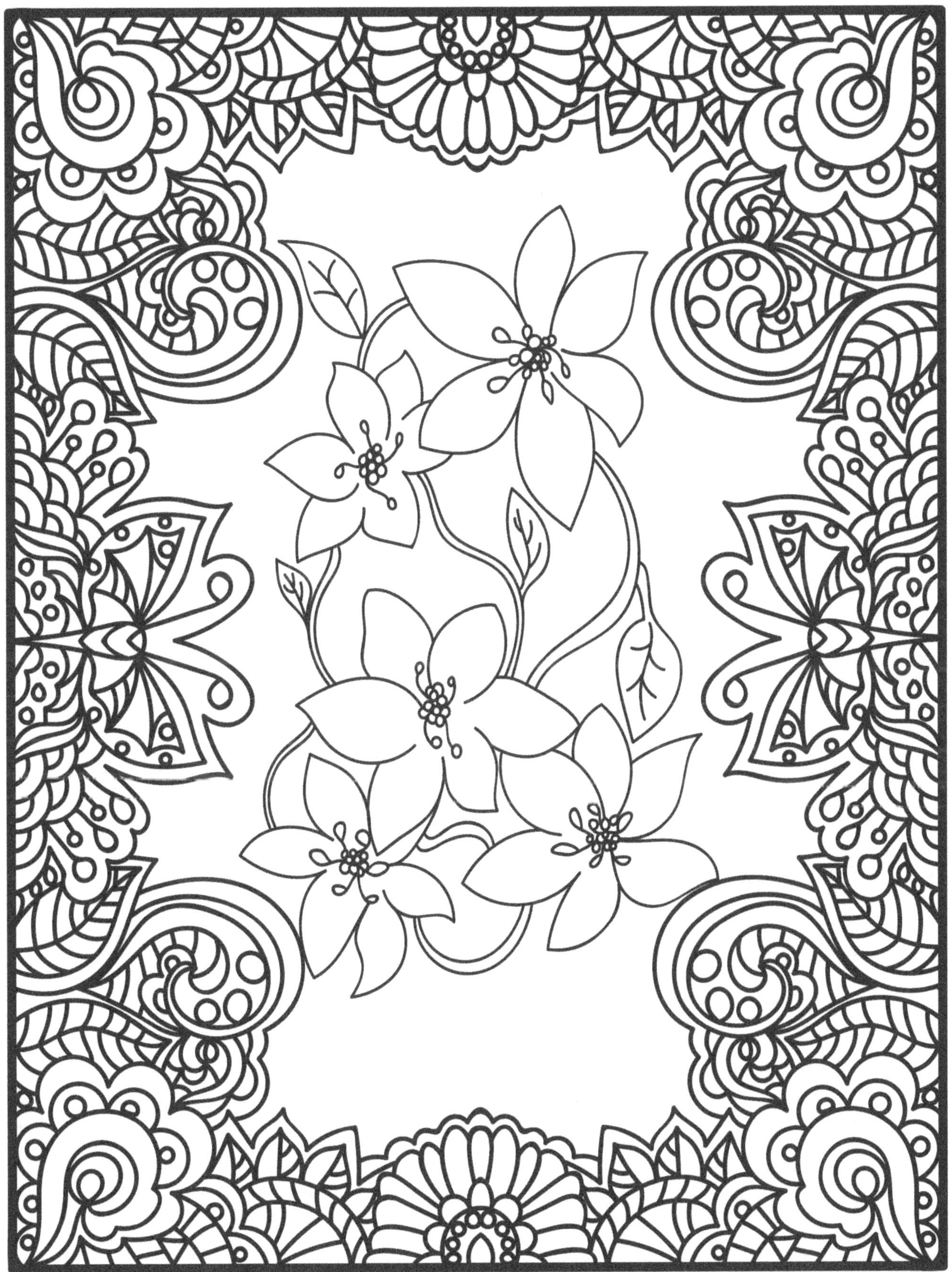

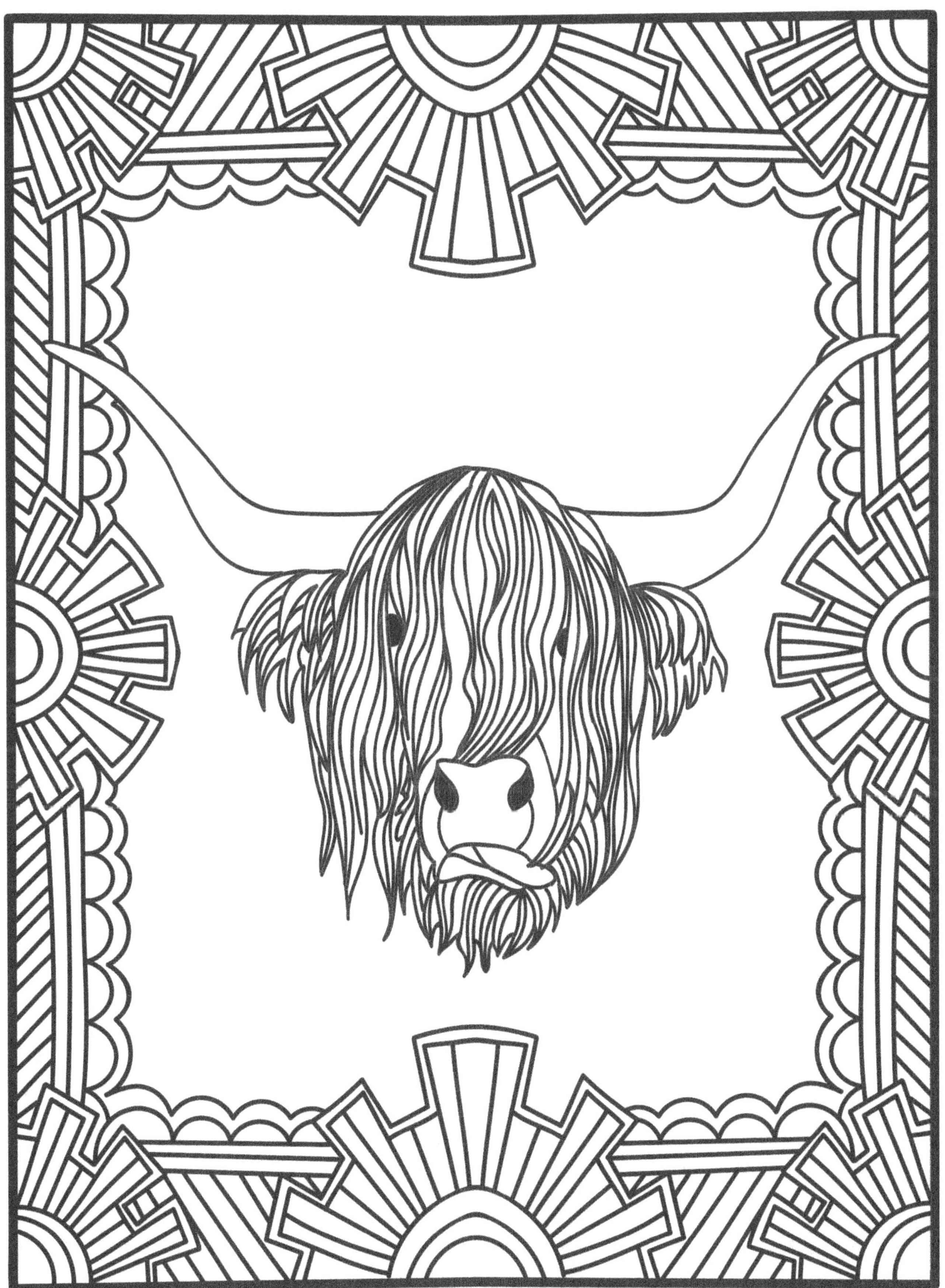

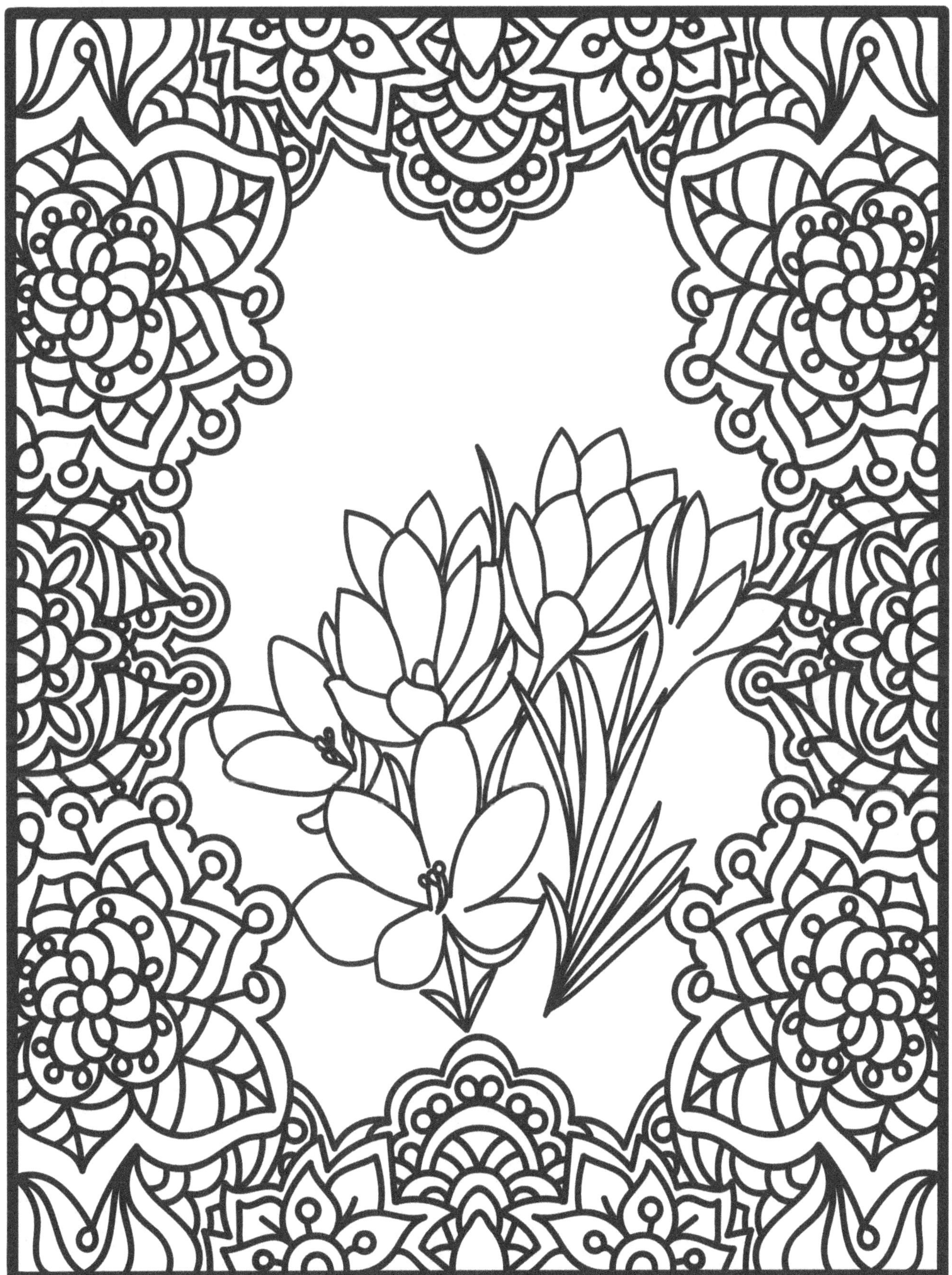

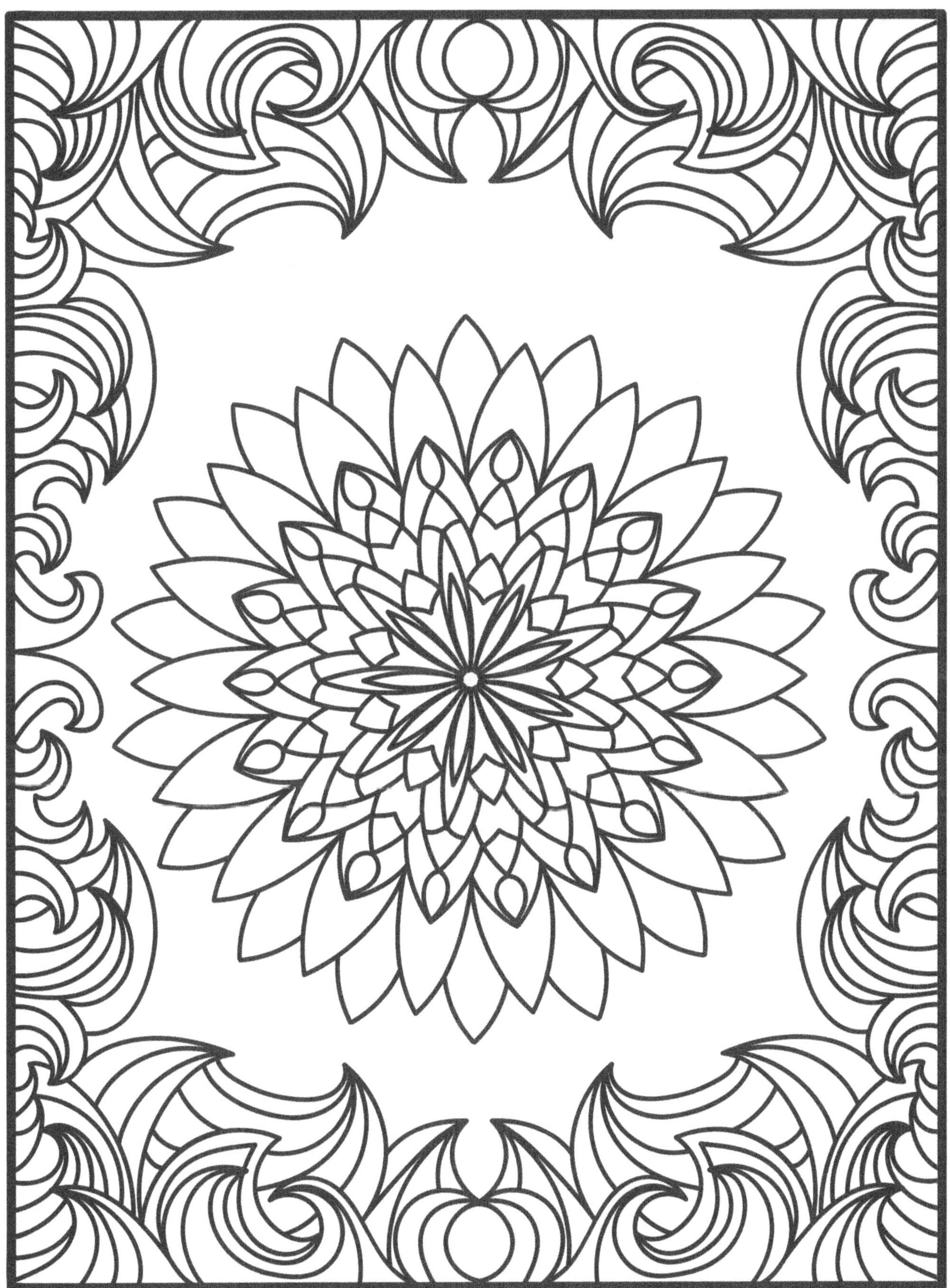

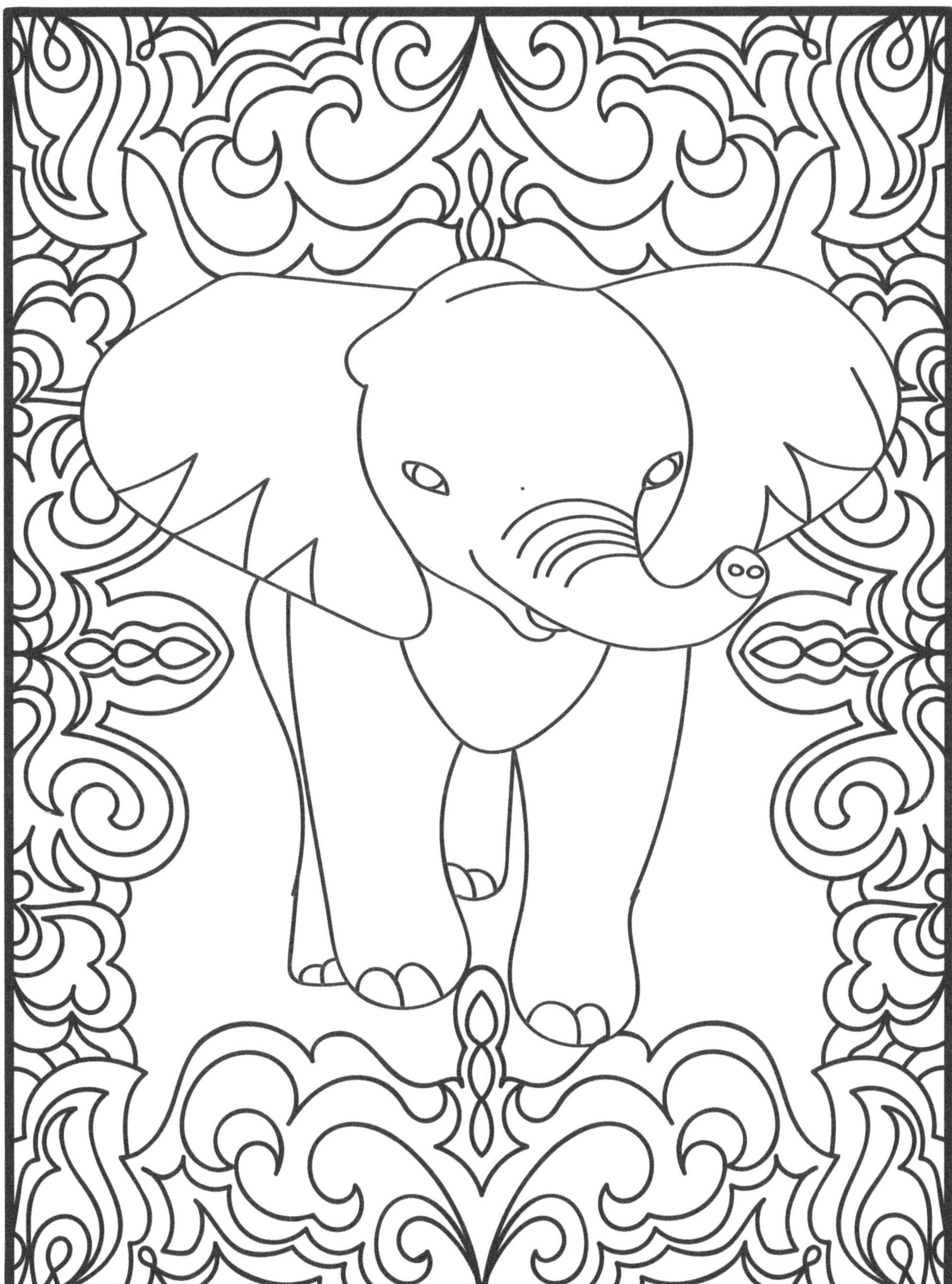

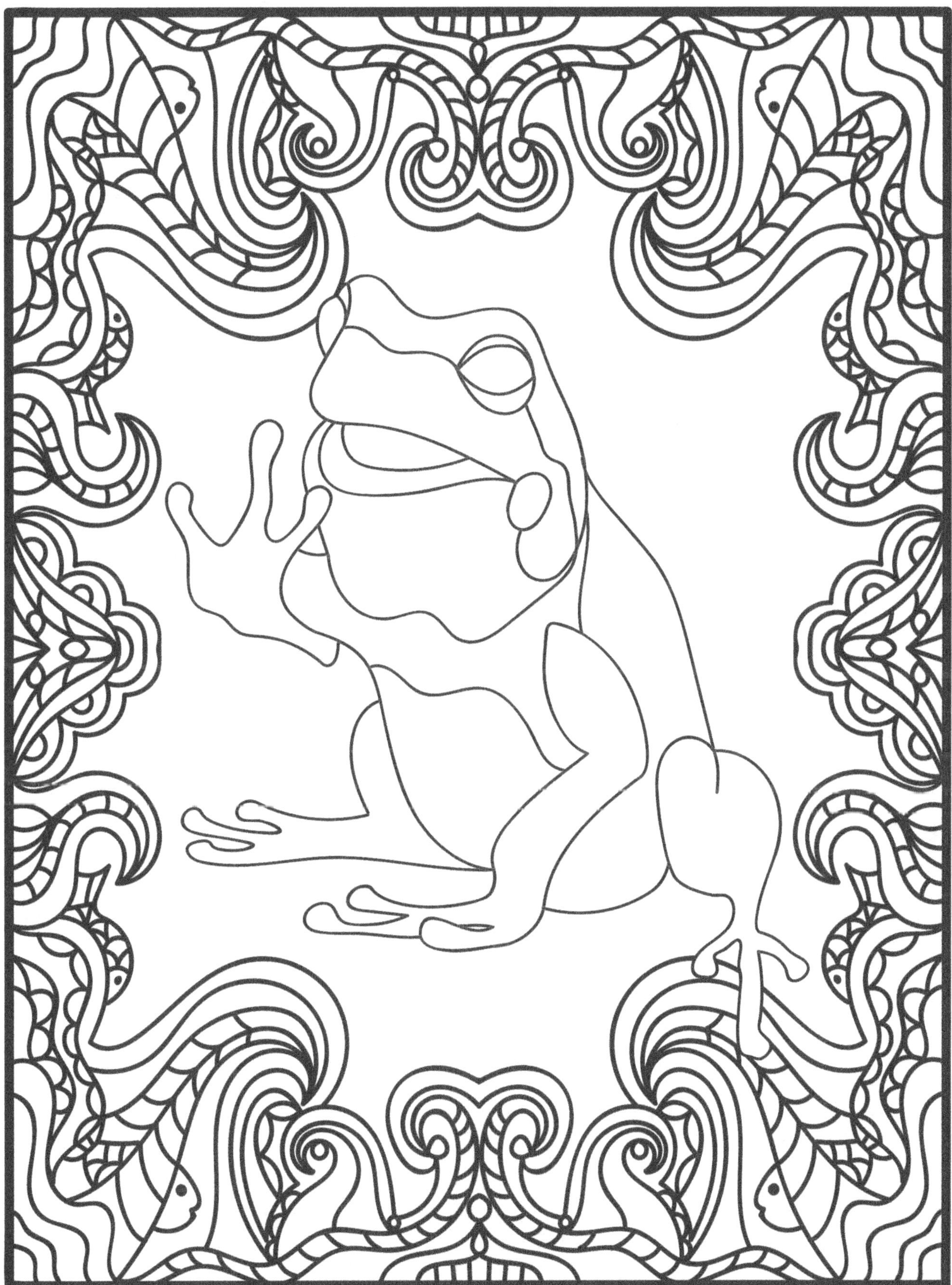

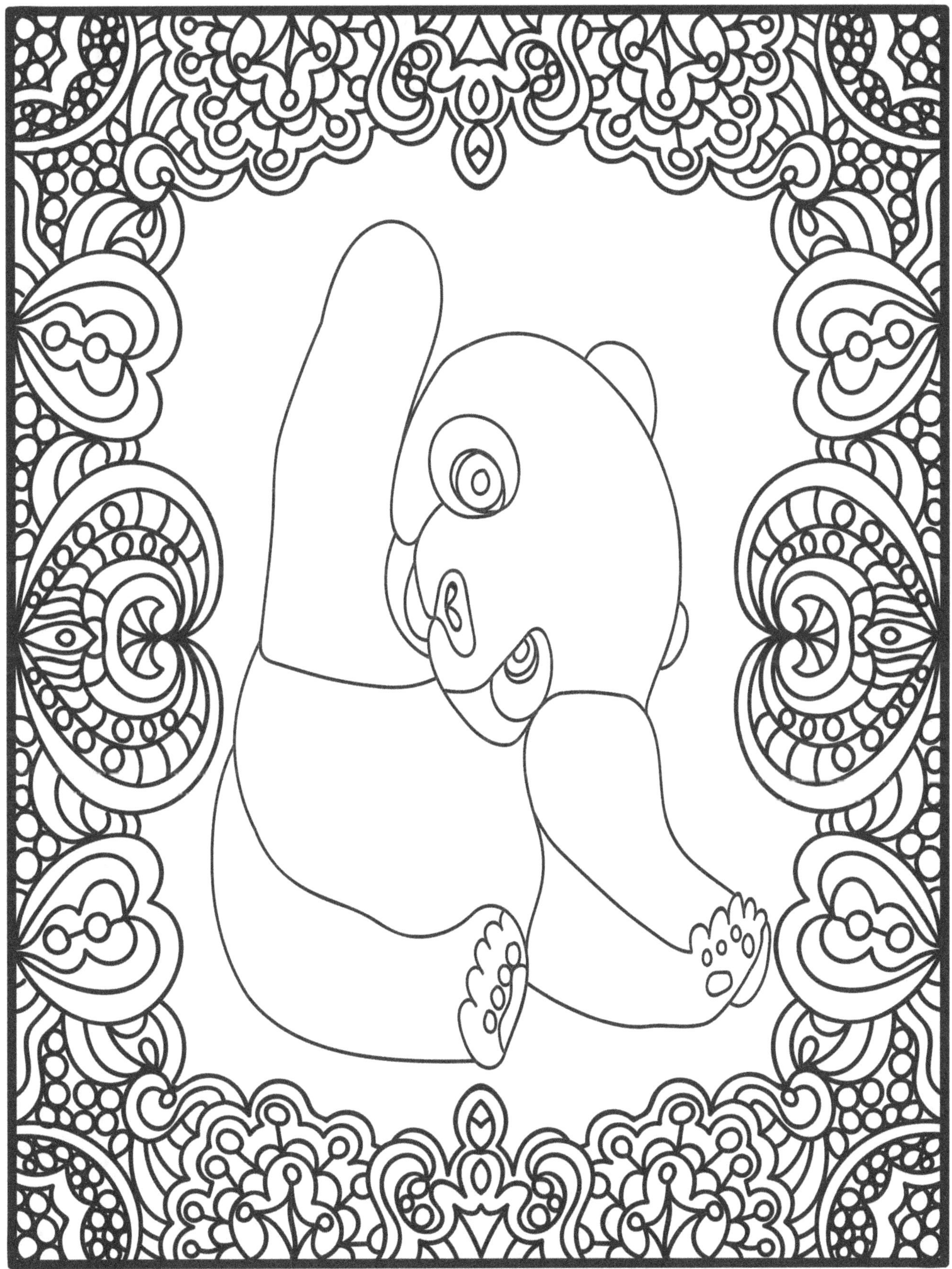

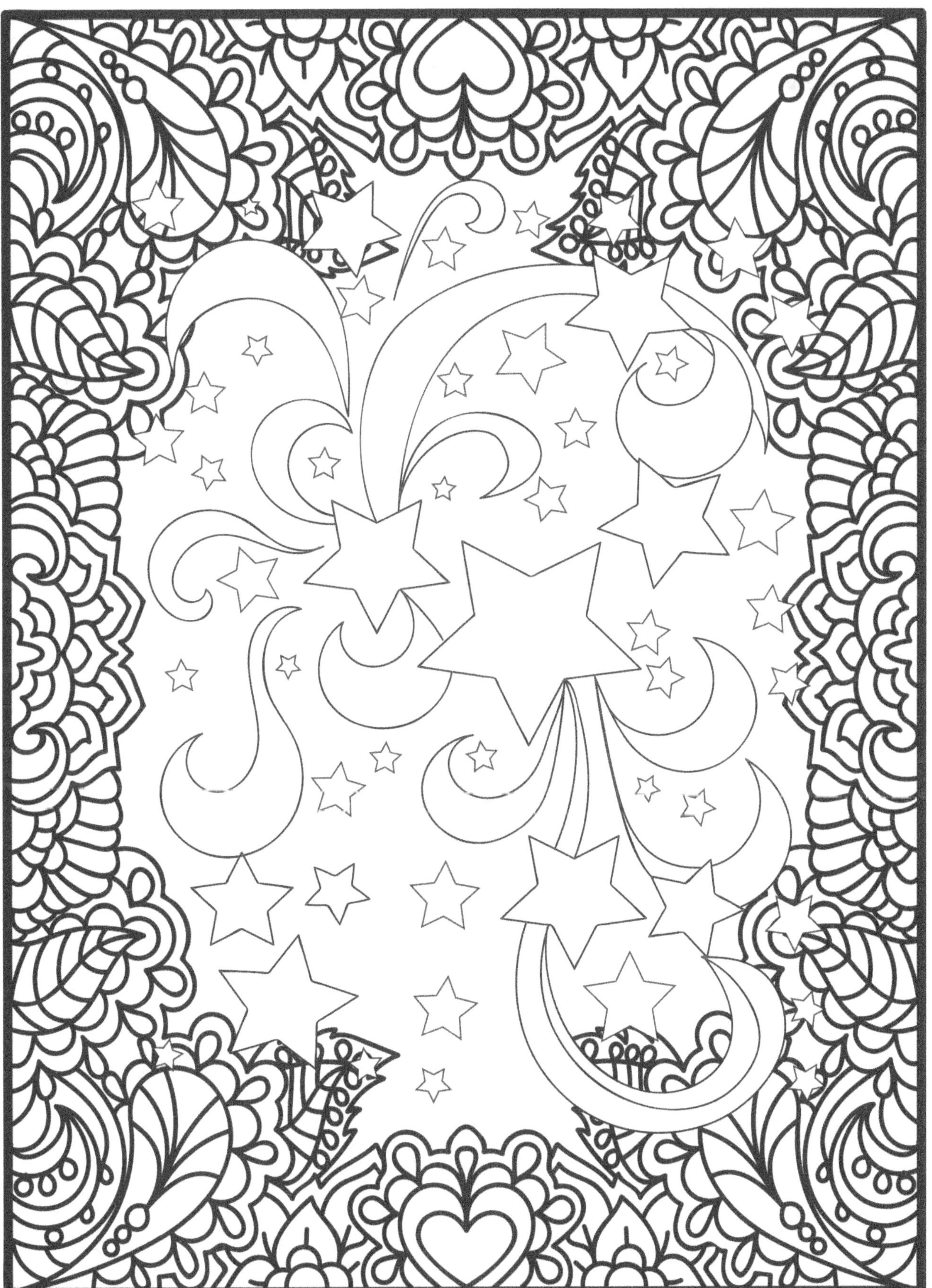

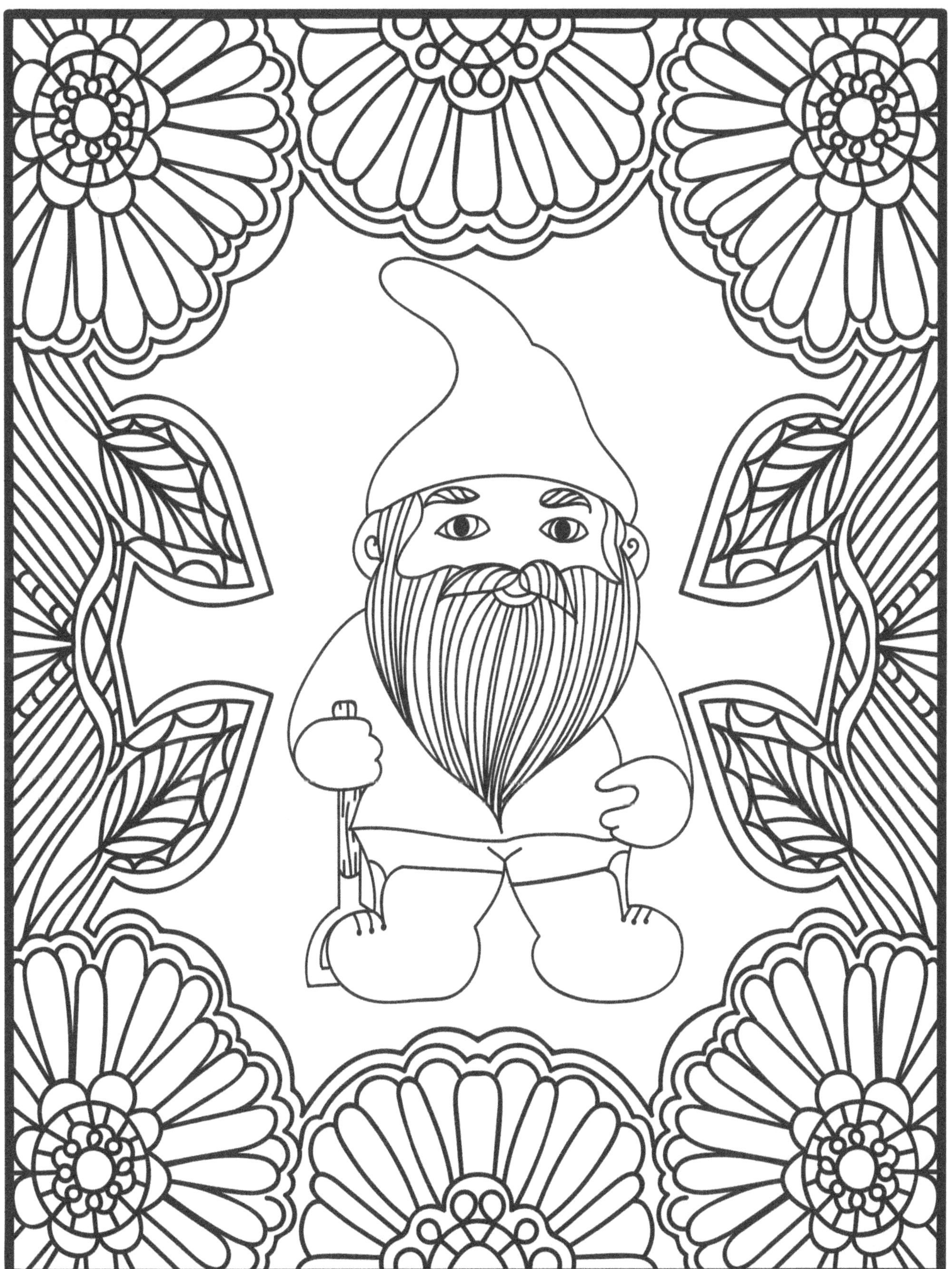

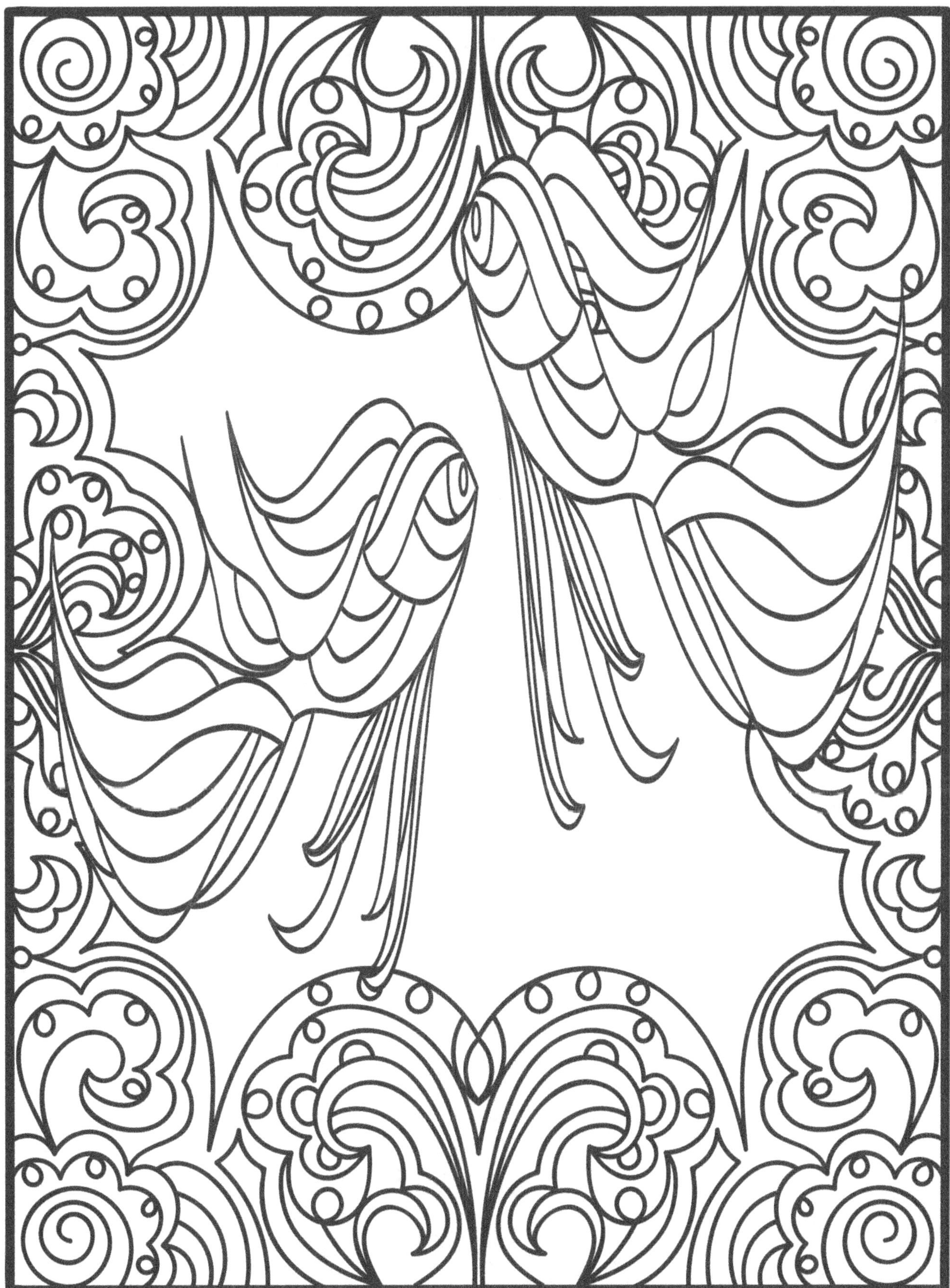

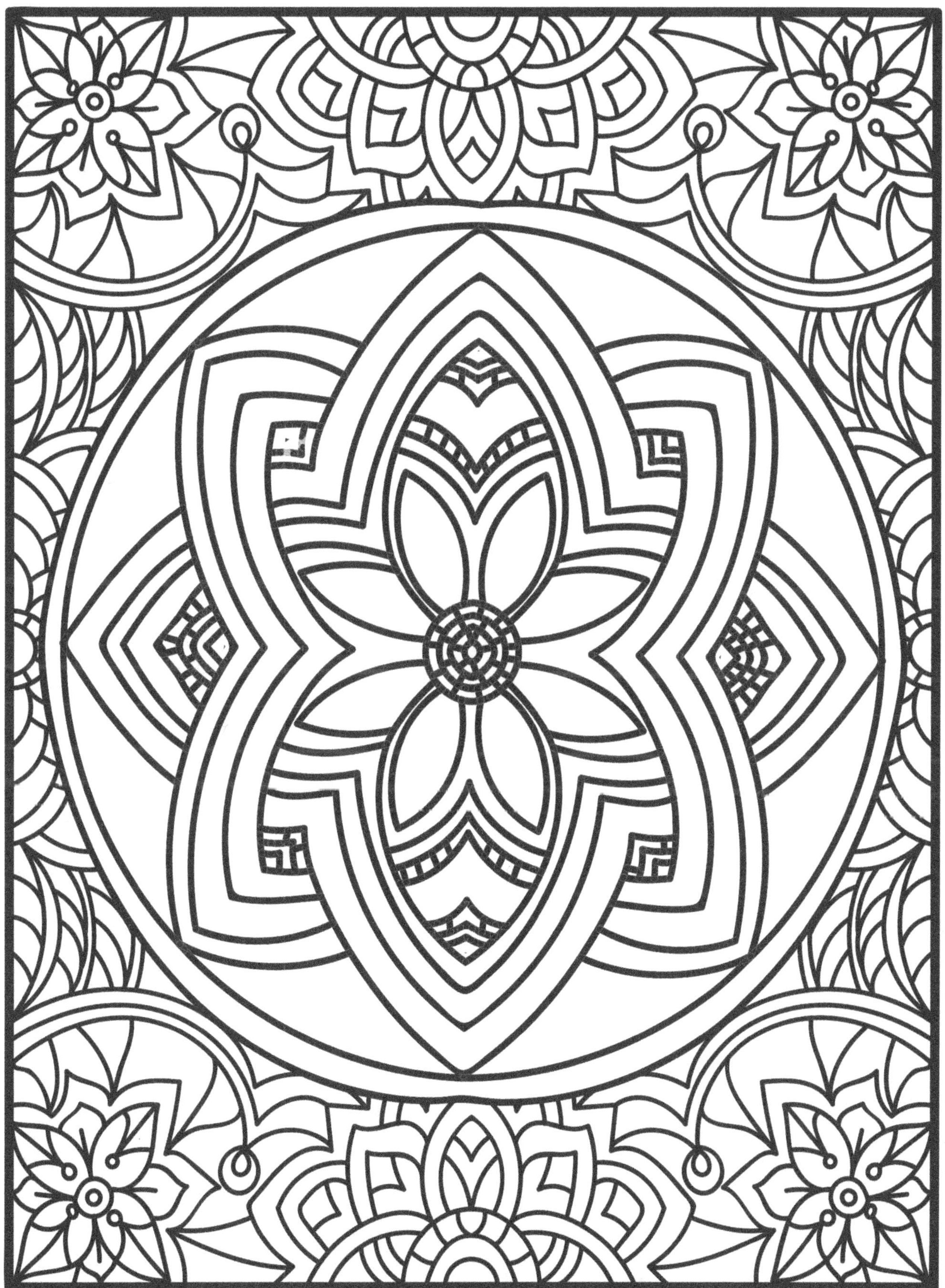

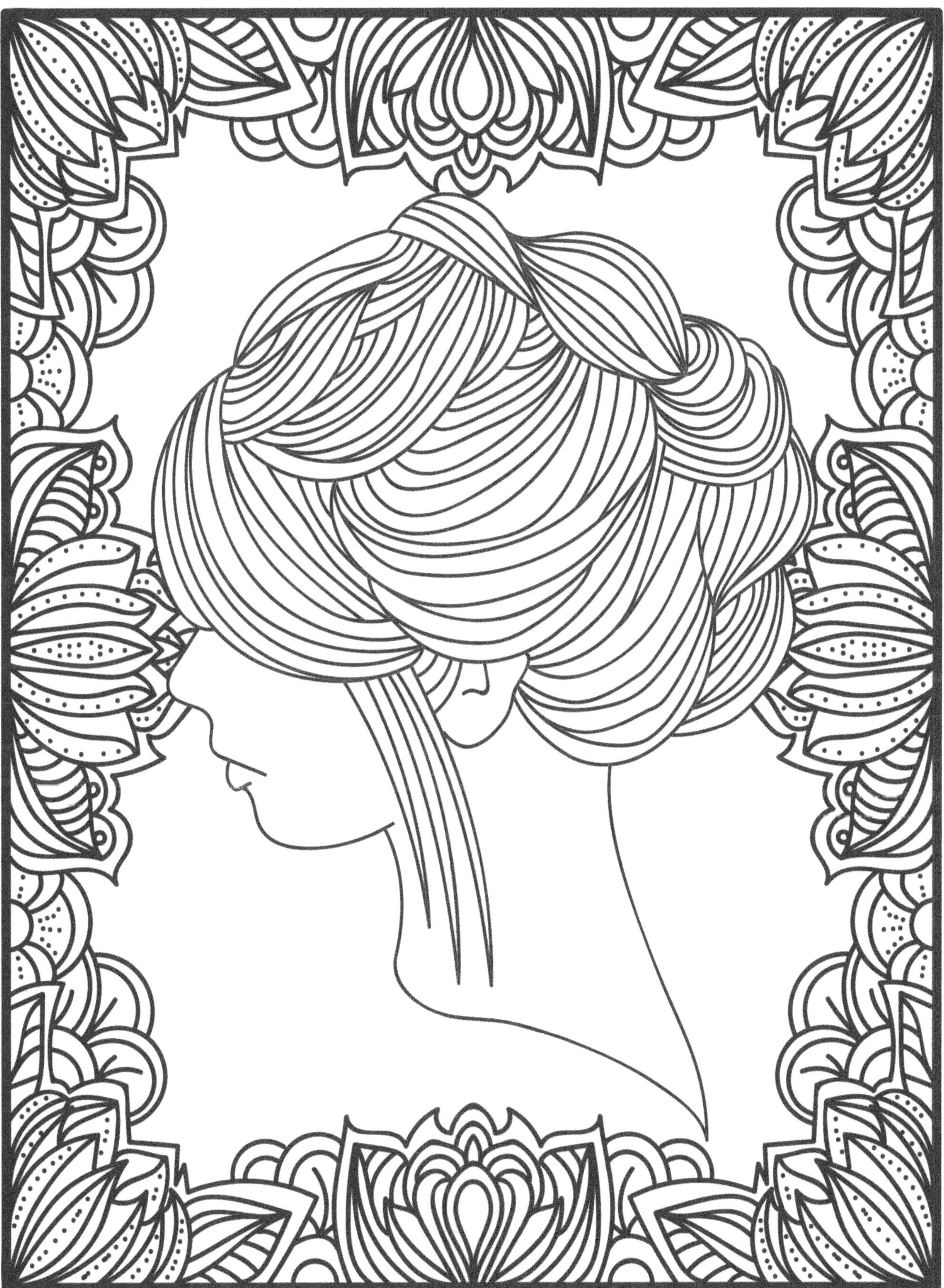

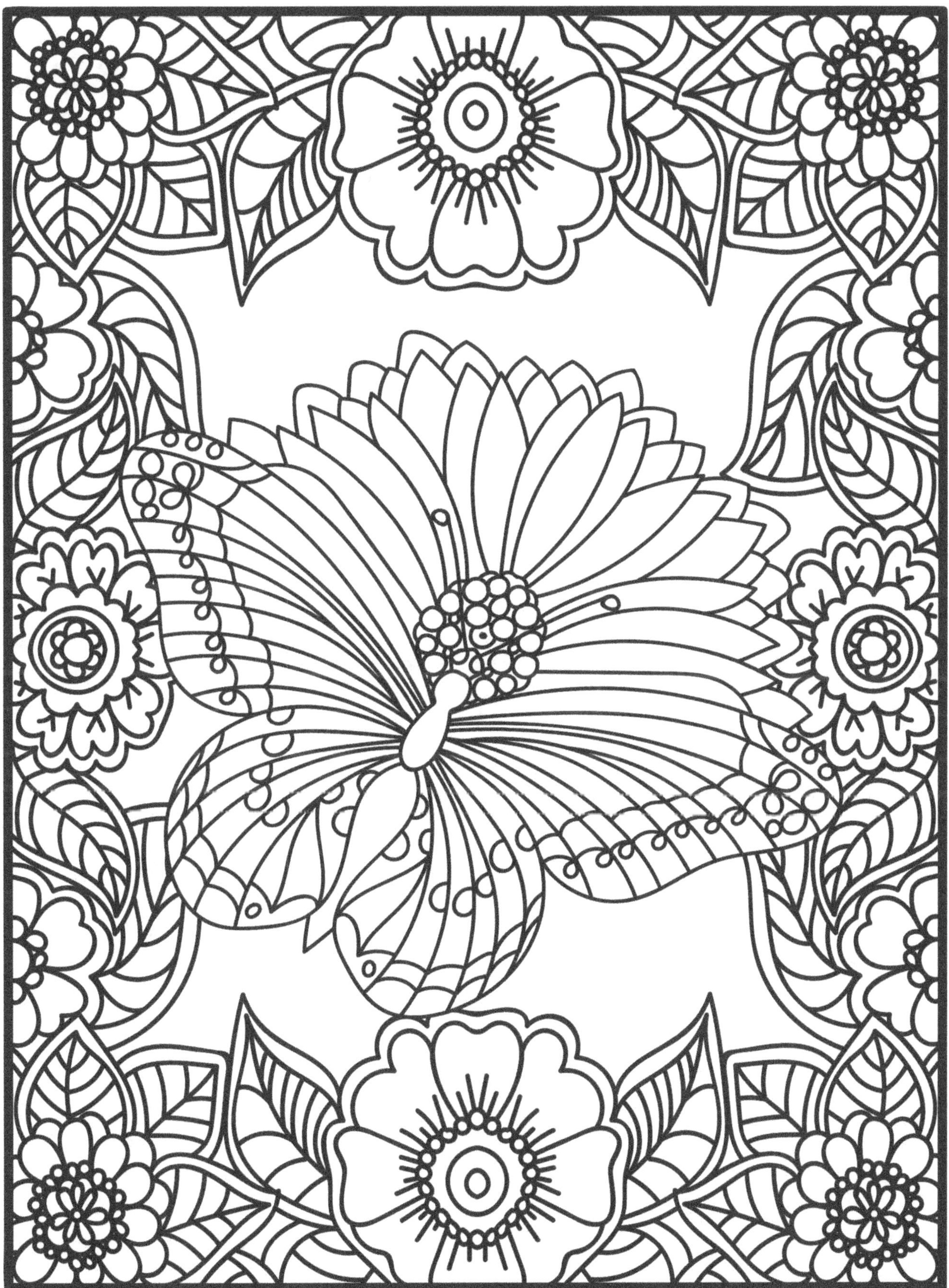

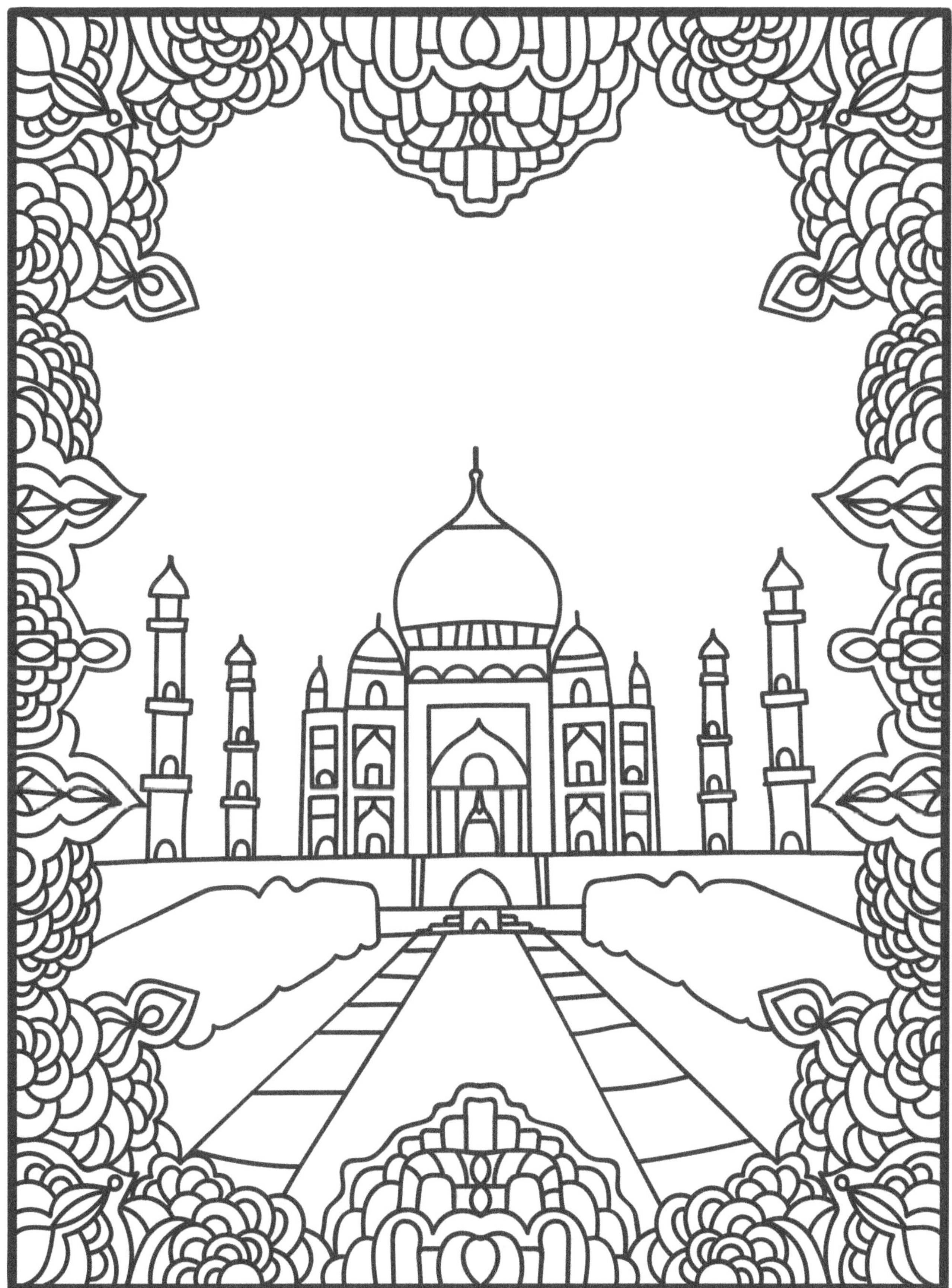

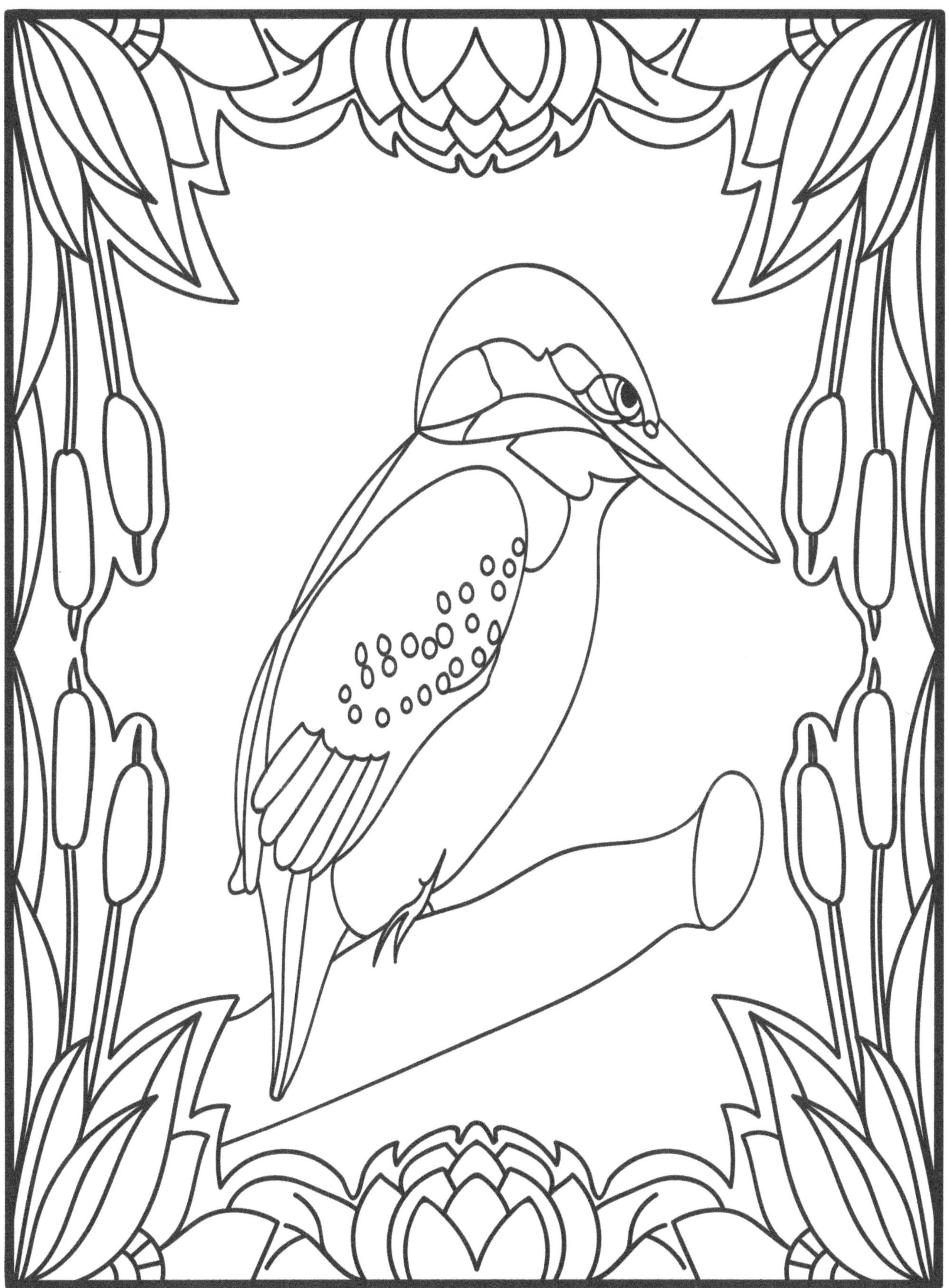

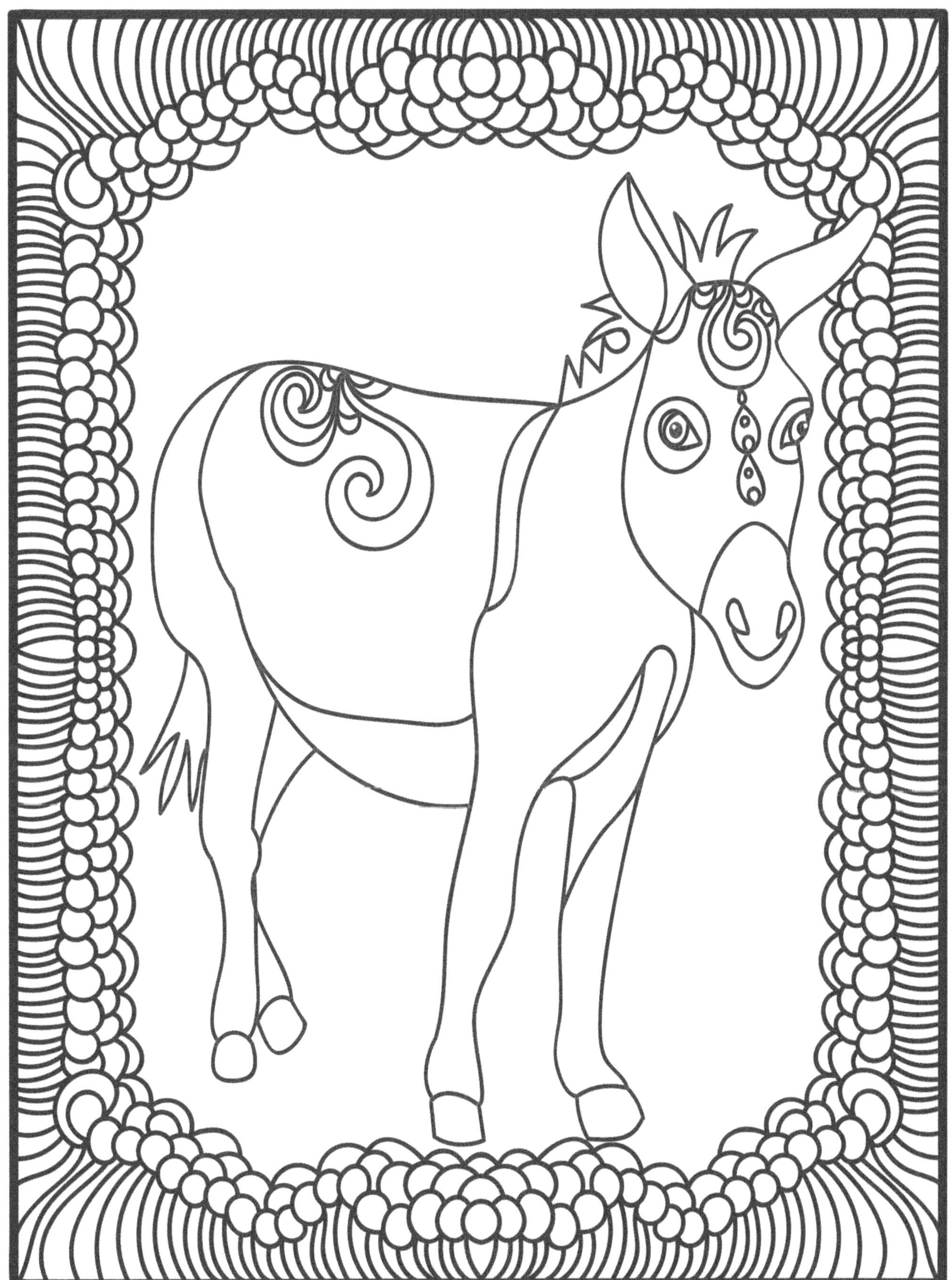

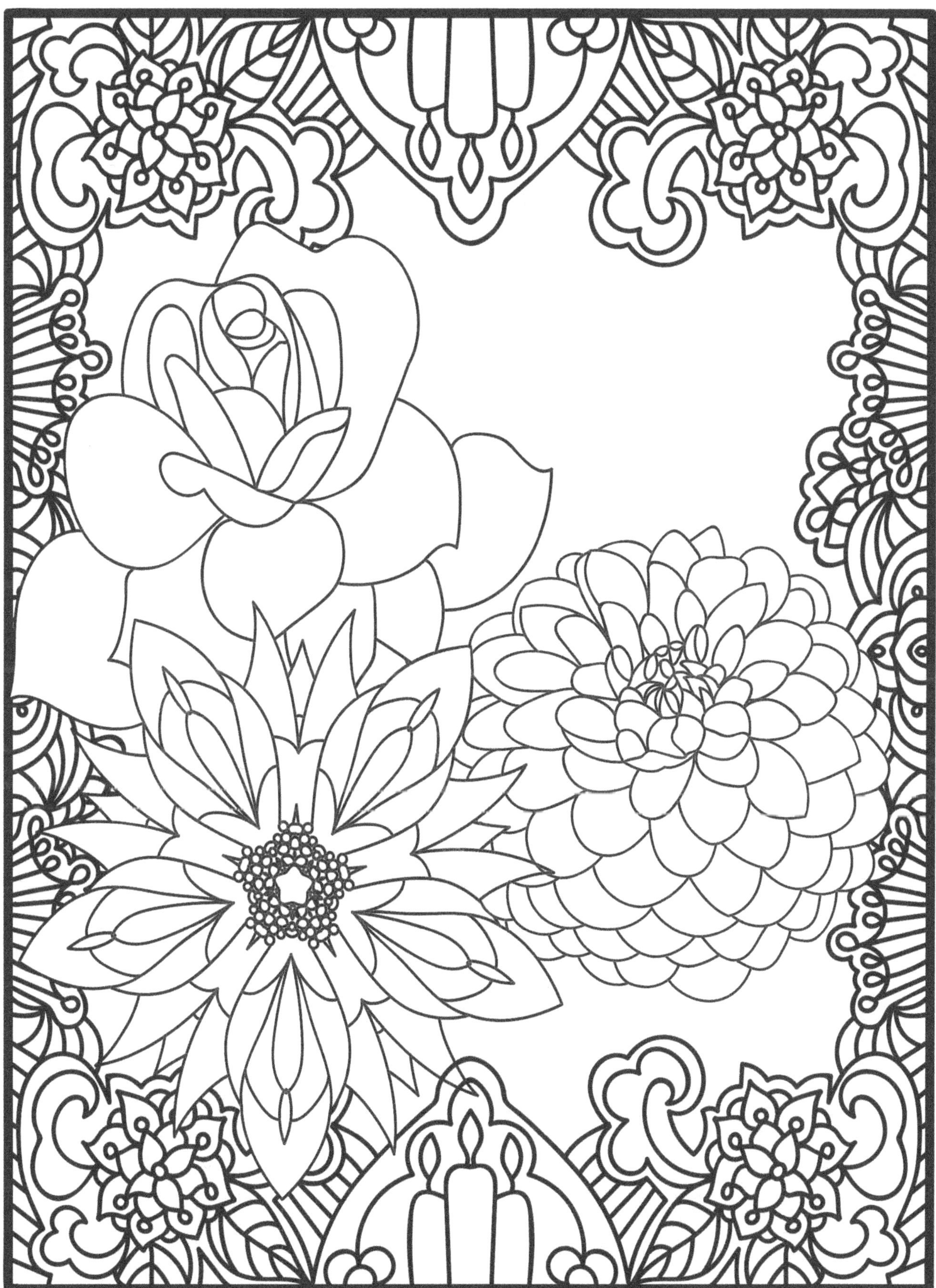

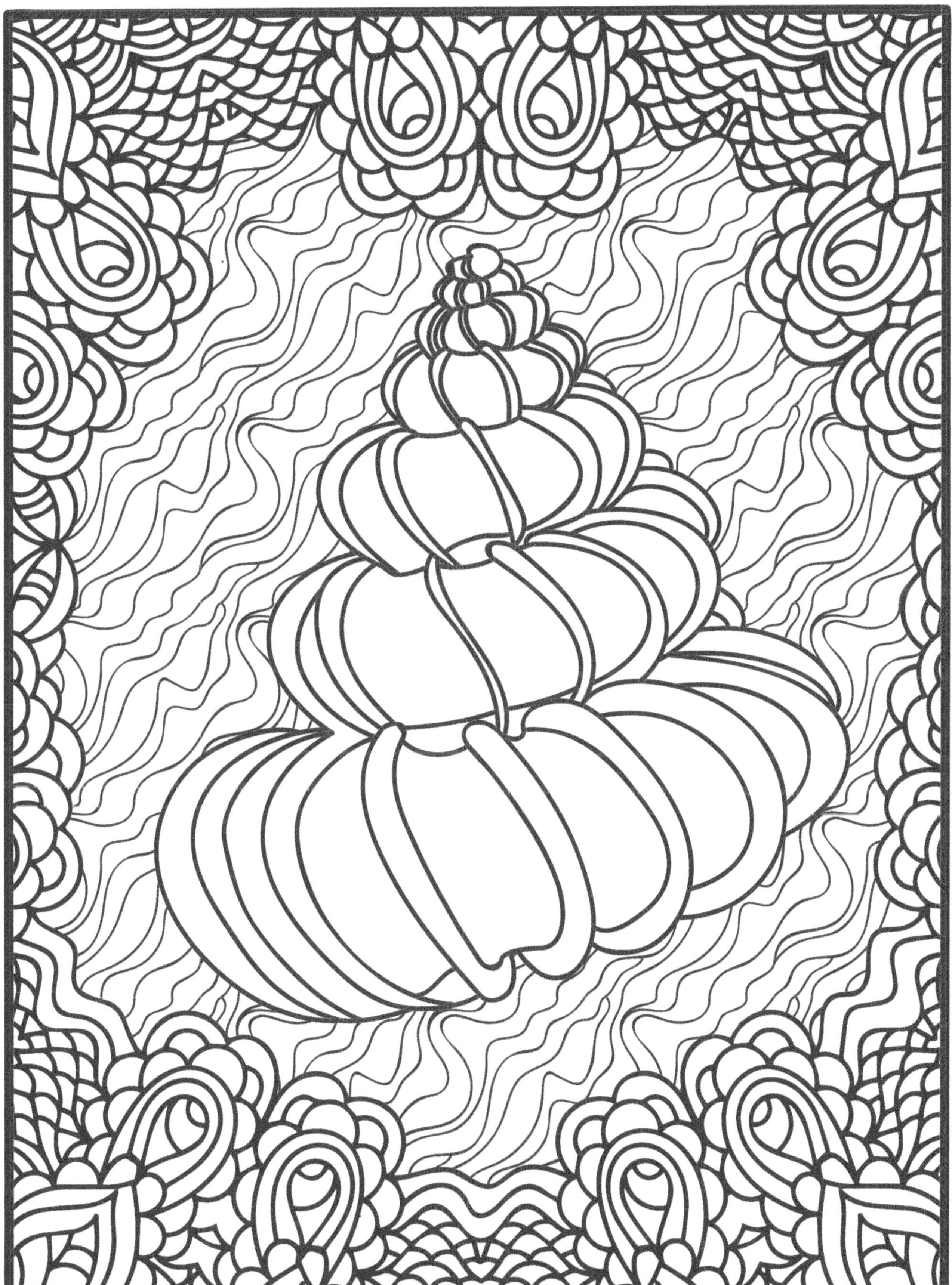

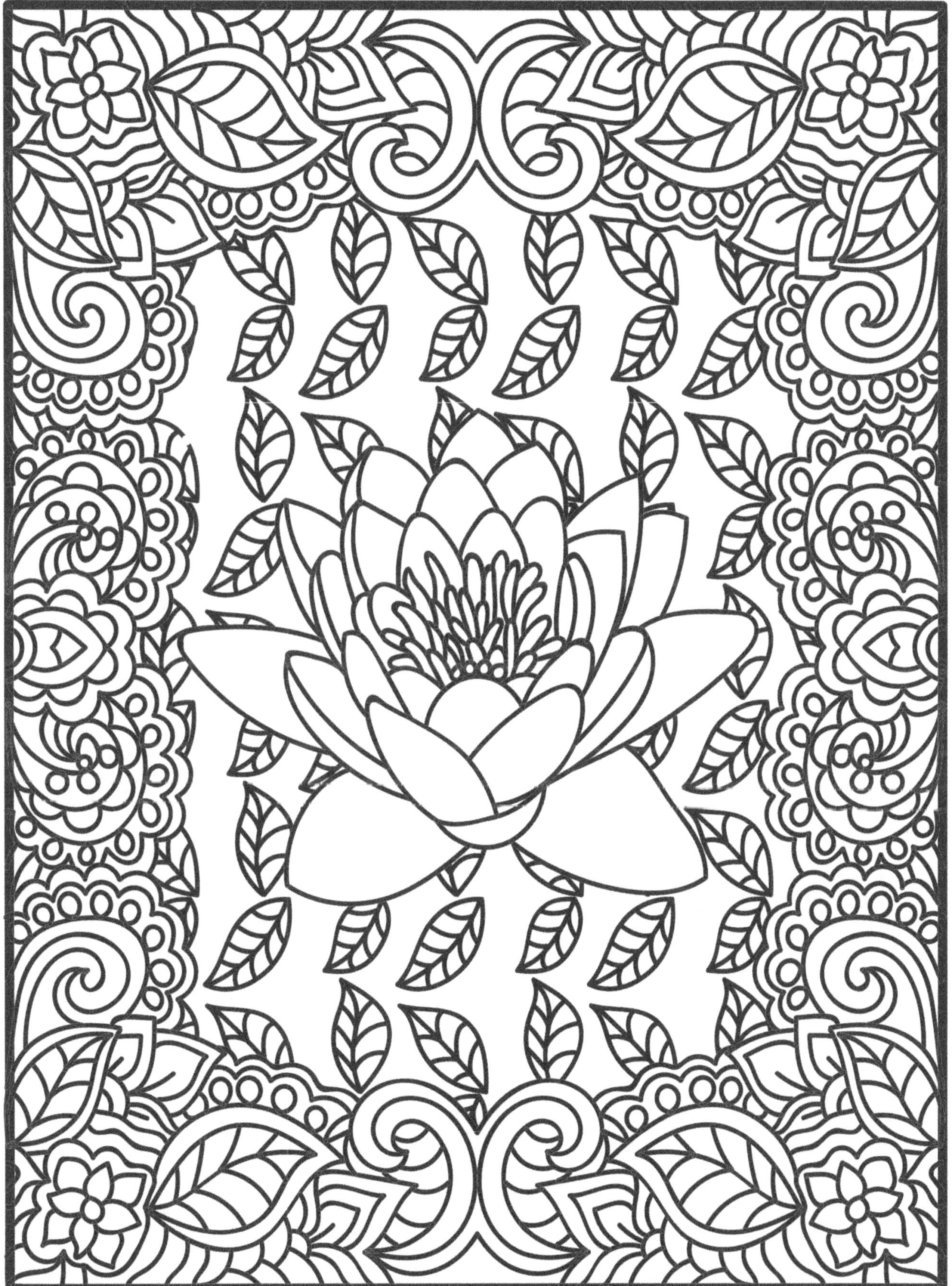

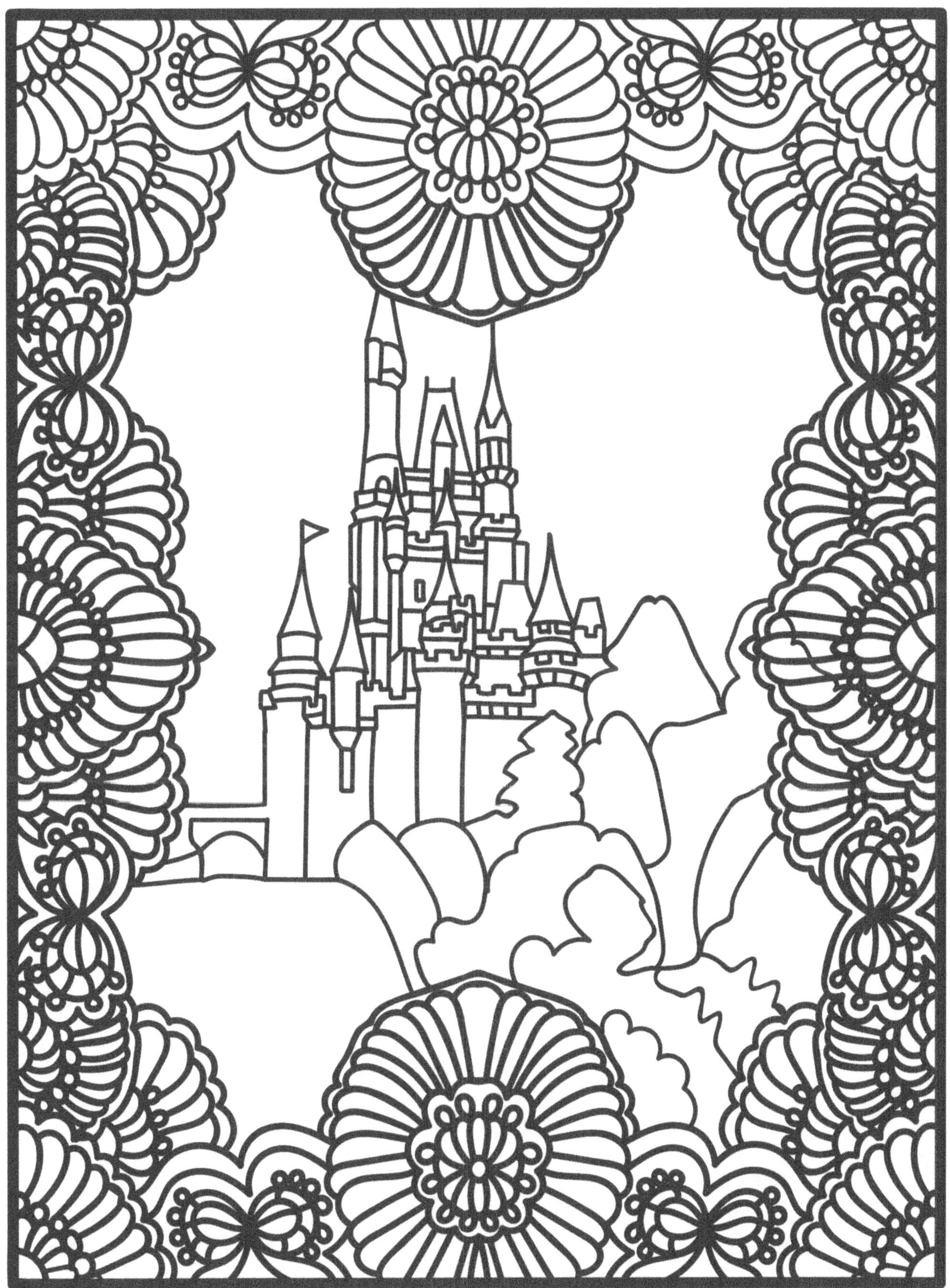

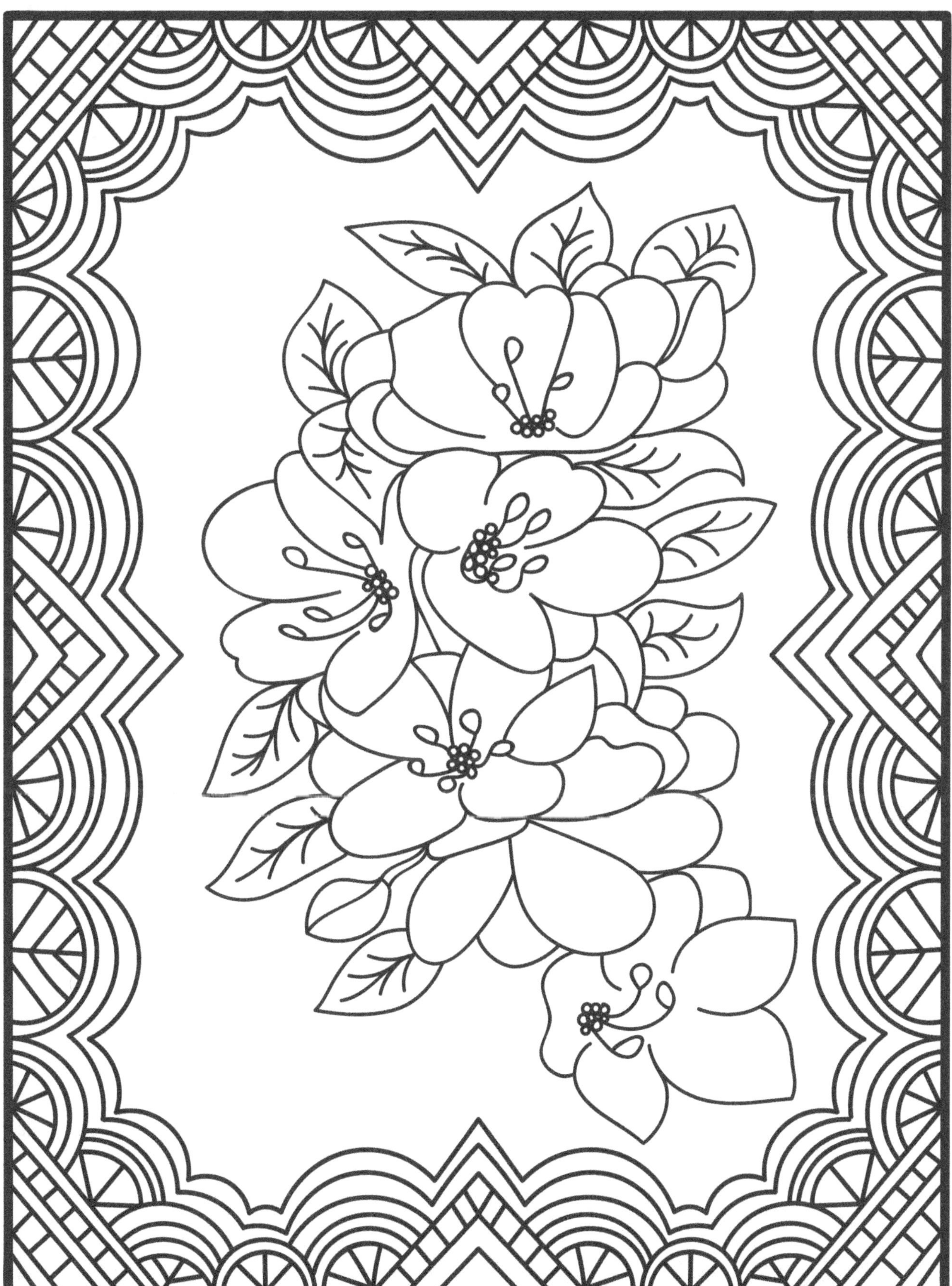

COLOR TEST PAGE

COLOR TEST PAGE